T0280020

Praise for Ou̶ ̶ ̶.̶.̶.̶.̶.̶.̶ng

"Through her storytelling, Cindy S. Lee provides practical, wise, and meaningful ways to embody a spirituality that centers Christ and roots us in the love and mystery of God. She reminds us that we are each a unique fabric and expression of God's beautiful tapestry. This book calls us as God's beloved to create sacred and inclusive spaces, see ourselves and each other as God does, share stories, and experience God's presence through our collective lives."

—**Mary Glenn**, assistant professor of the practice of chaplaincy and community development, Fuller Theological Seminary, and founding chaplain for the Los Angeles County District Attorney's Office

"This evocative and gracious book expands conversations on spiritual formation beyond the parameters of Western, white experience. As a scholar and practitioner, Cindy S. Lee interrogates the field with courage and insight. She offers the reader ways to break through colonized spaces, and she offers the field of spiritual formation subversive and creative ways to push beyond limited contextualization to a more expansive transformative vision. As a scholar of European descent, I found Lee's questions as integral to my own way of being in the world, and this work will undoubtedly enrich my own spiritual identity and practice. This welcoming book will help more people experience the transformative path of the sacred."

—**Sheryl A. Kujawa-Holbrook**, professor of practical theology and religious education, Claremont School of Theology

"Through her lens as an Asian American woman, Cindy S. Lee offers a contemplative approach with rich resources and practices to reimagine spiritual formation from its Westernized, white lens. Through her own experience and wisdom, along with the other BIPOC voices included in this volume, she provides a clear way toward a more robust spirituality to meet the diversity and challenges of our times. It's a powerful diversity, equity, inclusion, and justice treatise on spiritual formation."

—**Ravi Verma**, past council chair of
Spiritual Directors International

"I have been waiting for this book for a long time, even before I knew Cindy was writing it. As a practitioner and teacher of spiritual formation, I have struggled with the vacuum of stated context in spiritual formation literature. As a white woman processing my formation, I, too, need unforming. This thoughtful, well-written volume will go far to correct this. I will recommend this book often."

—**Jude Tiersma Watson**, senior associate professor
of urban mission, Fuller Theological Seminary

"*Our Unforming* is the breath of fresh air my body, mind, and soul crave. It has given me new insight and awareness as I continue my lifelong formation journey of 'uncluttering,' communing with God, co-journeying, and leading others as they do the same. Dr. Lee helps us see the need for new languages, orientations, and postures in spiritual formation. Drawing from her rich cultural heritage and wealth of knowledge, Lee helps us to begin our unforming of Western paradigms of formation that focus on progress, knowledge, and the individual.

"This work guides us to embrace orientations and postures that are grounded in the lived experiences and reality of our ancestors, passed down on the front porch, at the kitchen table, and in the living room. It gives BIPOC folks permission to embrace their own cultural heritage and postures they may have put down and abandoned in favor of Western paradigms that have been center stage. Lee draws us back to the heart of spiritual formation as she guides us into connecting and being formed by God as a way of being versus doing, both individually and communally.

"This book is a must-have for folks who lead others in spiritual formation—not as a how-to book, but as an invitation to deepen their own journey so they may be unformed and formed; so that they may guide and lead others in a more holistic, embodied, and authentic way. This book is needed for the church and its body, who have found themselves desolate and dry like the deer in Psalm 42, longing and thirsting for our living God to be present and near as we navigate the complex reality of our lives and society."

—**Tracey Shenell**, consultant, life coach, writer, speaker, and pastor

"This book has the power to set a new path for spiritual formation and vitality in the promise of a new humanity. In *Our Unforming*, Dr. Cindy S. Lee provides a liberating road for a spirituality for the global church by relinquishing the limitations and values of Western thinking. I have waited for a book like this to provide new perspectives, freedom, depth, and cultural sensitivity for a spiritual posture among non-Western Christians. Read this book and be challenged, renewed, and encouraged."

—**Wilmer Villacorta**, associate professor, Fuller Theological Seminary, and author of *Tug of War* and *Unmasking the Male Soul*

Our Unforming

Our
UN*form*ING

De-Westernizing
Spiritual Formation

Cindy S. Lee

Fortress Press
Minneapolis

To Ahma, my childhood companion

Contents

Part 3
Orientation 三 Collective   99

Acknowledgments

There is a part of me that longs to be a hermit, but I recognize that I am a better me because of my loving community.

To my family, *all* of my family: thank you for your everloving presence in my life. I would not be who I am today without all the meals we share together.

To Saraiah and Ayra: you keep me grounded and humble because you knew me when I hated school and got in trouble for sleeping in class. Your presences are a source of great comfort to me, and I look forward to when we live in a retirement home together.

To Angel, Christine, Debi, Melinda, Tracey: you read these words and affirmed that these words were worth putting out there. Each time I doubted myself, you believed in me. Thank you for your constant words of encouragement along the way. They meant so much more to me than you know.

To my editor, Beth, and the team at Fortress Press whose names I may not know: thank you for all the ways you use your amazing gifts to birth books. And thank you for taking a risk and believing in this book.

INTRODUCTION

For most of my life, I've been driven by a deep, insatiable hunger for God that has never actually gone away. I am not satisfied with simply knowing the breadth of God, but I want to continually experience the very depths of God. My longings have led me to many rich Christian spiritual traditions from the Desert Mothers and Fathers, to Benedictine hospitality, to Celtic pilgrimages, to Ignatian spiritual exercises, to practices of contemplation. In all my studies and explorations of Christian spirituality, however, it suddenly dawned on me one day that as much as I esteem the many saints and mystics of our faith . . . very few of them look like me.

For all my life, I've read books on spiritual formation written by white authors and internalized their experiences of God as the norm and even as the authority. In recent centuries, our spiritual formation resources and teachings have primarily come from Western spiritual traditions. In that process, Western voices have generalized what spiritual formation is for all of us. The way we teach formation in the church is heavily influenced by Western values—such as individuality, dualism, and linear thinking—and Western history like colonialism, the Enlightenment, and industrialization. Even the African roots of early church fathers and mothers have often been ignored when interpreted through a white male lens.

As I get older and become more comfortable in my own skin, I sense more and more a discontinuity in my soul. In trying to pursue the Christian faith, I am continually asked to conform to a Western way of being and behaving. When I travel to Christian monasteries and retreat centers, I find myself frequently staring at the images of Western saints and white Jesus. My experience in the church is not much different when I look at who's teaching from the stage or sitting in leadership. I have been seeking answers from institutions not made with people like me in mind.

You are reading a book on Christian spirituality by an Asian American author. I hope, though, that you don't categorize or marginalize my writing as "other" or as "only for Asians." Instead, I hope that you can receive my experiences of the sacred as one layer of our collective human experience of God. I want to untangle and de-westernize the ways my soul has been distorted by the disproportionate influence of Western authority in the church. This does not mean disregarding our long and rich history of Christian spiritual traditions. Rather, we need to recognize that our current understanding of spiritual formation is limited because it was developed under a dominant Western cultural tradition.

Spirituality, however, is not static and fixed. Far from it. The spiritual life is always transforming. In this way, spirituality should reflect a multiplicity of layered human experiences of God. Our collective soul as a church will atrophy if one culture or tradition holds the power and control over what is taught and practiced in the church. When we are limited by a Western vocabulary, we limit God. We need to expand our vocabulary to hold one another's sacred experiences so we can expand and deepen our experiences in God together.

I believe we need a more robust spirituality for our times. Our spiritual practices need to be reimagined as our communities become increasingly diverse. We need a spirituality not detached from reality but one that takes seriously the injustices and disparities of our societies. We also need to be re-formed in order to discover the sacred in one another. Sadly, voices are missing from this conversation. We need to hear from one another and make space for one another so we can evolve and mature into a more dynamic spiritual community.

What Is Spirituality?

Spirituality, the divine-human relationship, starts with an ache. Our souls ache each time we recognize that there is something missing in our experiences of the sacred. I hope that as Christians we never lose our deep aches, no matter how long we have been in the church, because that ache represents the human search for God. I believe that people of color also ache, because our cultural experiences of the sacred that we may practice in our homes or in our communities have not been adequately reflected in the church. Even more, we ache each time we try to reconcile the God we believe in with the racism, sexism, and homophobia we experience in the church from people who claim to believe in the same God.

Whereas theology attempts to figure out and articulate what we *know* about God, spirituality refers to what we *experience* of God. This means that spirituality takes all our human experiences seriously, because we need to bring our full selves in order to meet with God. Howard Thurman writes that whenever we meet with God, we carry the "smell of life on us."[1] We draw from the depths of our complicated emotions, weary bodies, family history, cultural experiences, frustrations with work, longings for true community, and even our everyday, mundane routines. In spirituality, we bring all of our humanness—broken, smelly, and beautiful—before God, just as God comes with all Godness to meet with us. *Spiritual formation*, then, refers to the transformation that happens in us as we encounter God again and again and again. Spiritual formation includes all the practical ways we try to clear the clutter in our souls in order to meet with God and hear from God.

Because the term *spiritual formation* can be deceptive, implying that we only need to engage with spiritual things, I like to think of spiritual formation as human formation. We live in a world that constantly devalues and distorts our humanness. Sitting with God teaches us how to see ourselves and others as sacred. This is human formation. I believe Western ways of spiritual formation have failed to form us as human beings. Historically, the church prioritized preparing souls for the afterlife but failed to form us to be healthy human beings in this life. The church overemphasized teaching the right beliefs but, in doing so, failed to form us to be people who ask God questions. If we don't learn to ask God questions, we don't allow God to reveal Godself to us but allow others to define God for us. Spiritual formation is the inner transformation we need to be better human beings.

What Is the Soul?

The word *soul* is a fuzzy term that is hard to grasp and define with words, but we all intuitively experience our souls. I find it helpful to think of the soul not as a being or object but as a space. The soul is the space where your sacred self dwells. This means your soul is also the space of prayer—where your most honest, sacred self meets with God. Rather than thinking of prayer as an activity or practice, I like to think of it as sharing space with God. Sometimes in prayer, we have conversations with the Spirit, and on the days when we're not sure what to say, we may simply sit in silence together. In that space, God sees us clearly. And on the good days, we see God clearly too.

Sometimes only you and God share that space. But when we experience deep relationships and true community, we allow others into that space too. Much goes on in this inner space called the soul. Our inner thoughts can run a hundred miles an hour and make us feel distracted. Sometimes our fears and anxieties can overwhelm our space. Sometimes we may resist entering that space when we know there's a tough conversation we need to have with God. In that space, our souls hold our deepest desires, which other people may never see and of which even we may be unaware. When we yearn to hear from God, the soul is where the whispers of the Spirit reverberate. Because our souls can get distracted by all the voices fighting for our attention, the space of our souls can be healthy or unhealthy. When our souls are healthy, we have a clear view of ourselves and God. When they are unhealthy, our views of self and God become distorted.

As a spiritual director, my role is to create a physical space that models the soul space. I set the room and create a space for my directees to sit with the divine Creator. Sometimes I light a candle to represent the presence of Spirit in the room, but it is always up to the directee to come into the space with their sacred self. I have the privilege and honor of being invited into their intimate soul space to listen to and with them. Together, we wait patiently as we listen for how the Spirit may be moving through each season of life. We also listen for how my directee is becoming more fully their sacred self.

The soul is intricately tied to our bodies, minds, and emotions. In our being, we carry a microcosm of the triune God. We are body, mind, and soul, just as the Trinity is a unity of Christ, Creator, and Spirit. Thus, we can experience our bodies, minds, and souls as distinct, but we integrate all three to actually experience ourselves as one being. How we perceive the triune God can reflect how we perceive our own bodies. In the same way we sometimes overemphasize one person of the Trinity and neglect the others, we may overemphasize or neglect parts of ourselves. We dissect body, mind, and soul into separate, disconnected entities. In *Dancing with God*, womanist theologian Karen Baker-Fletcher explains that the Eastern church understands the Trinity as three *relations* or *movements* in one nature.[2] Baker-Fletcher writes, "God, who is three *hypostases* or *relations* in one nature, is like three distinct dancers who make up one dynamic dance." Movement in one causes movement in the others. In the same way, our selves as body, mind, and soul are not separate entities but are intricately connected. When our bodies are weary, our souls will inevitably be weary. When we overemphasize the mind, our bodies and souls will be neglected. When our bodies breathe oxygen deep into our lungs, our souls expand too. Emotions are actually experienced in all three. When our emotions are wounded, our bodies, minds, and souls will all feel the stress. When I speak about the soul, then, I am just as much referring to its connection to the mind, body, and emotions as vice versa. We are meant to experience ourselves as a whole and not in parts.

Unforming and Re-forming

When our views of God and self are blurred, our bodies, minds, and emotions will all feel the strain. Thus the spiritual life requires a continuous cycle of unforming and re-forming. Unforming is the spiritual process of clearing out the clutter and the cobwebs that build up in us over time and prevent us from experiencing the sacred. This includes all the ways we become distracted by the busyness of life and all the unprocessed emotions that build up in us over time. We also unform the false ways this world has taught us or expects us to act in a system of patriarchy and whiteness. We unform our tendencies toward productivity and constant activity. In the unforming work, God addresses our fears, anxieties, griefs, and traumas. This unforming may even include our experiences in the church—that is, our beliefs, traditions, teachings, and discipleship. As we unform, we particularly need to address the harm of Western colonialism in the church. Unforming can sometimes be hard and painful, but it requires us to participate with the Spirit in the process of clearing out. Thankfully, as we are brought bare before God, God comes with all tenderness and compassion to meet with us in this unforming work.

Racism also needs to be addressed in our unforming. Racism is not only a systemic issue but a spiritual issue, because it distorts our souls. Black, Indigenous, and people of color (BIPOC) recognize we are harmed—distorted—not only by overt racist acts but also by the constant stress of messages in the media and the experiences of microaggression and gaslighting in the workplace and in the church. We get worn down by the extra effort needed to navigate in white spaces and manage our fears.

Slowly, the self becomes diminished, and our voices are suppressed. We become very small in our soul space. For BIPOC communities, unforming is just as healing as forming. We need to unlearn the practices, actions, and teachings of patriarchy and colonization that are ingrained in our bodies and habits. People of color in the church need to unform the ways we've disregarded our own cultural identities in order to conform to the Western values of the church.

Further, just as racism distorts the self-image of those oppressed by the dominant society, it equally distorts the souls of the perpetrators and the bystanders who remain silent. As Desmond Tutu famously said, "When I dehumanize you, I inexorably dehumanize myself."[3] When fear of the other festers, we can no longer see ourselves or God clearly.

We engage in continual unforming so that we can make space in ourselves for the Spirit to do new work in us. The work of re-forming, then, is the spirit-inspired movement of dreaming and imagining how our souls could be formed differently, especially if we are paying attention to other experiences of God. To re-form our souls, we need to adopt the practice of asking "What if?" What if when Western missionaries had set out to other lands, they had gone to learn and listen instead of colonize and convert? How might our liturgies look different today? What if the leaders of denominations and Christian organizations intentionally transferred power to leaders of color? How would our communities look different today? What if our cultural stories and traditions inform our experiences of God? How would our spiritual practices be different? As we ask these "what if" questions, I am hopeful that it's not too late to find out. Re-forming is a communal practice of listening to one another and listening for the Spirit together.

I believe we will discover in this century how our communities can be transformed when women, LGBTQI+, and BIPOC spiritual leaders become our teachers.

The work of re-forming our souls is important. I think we need a different spirituality for our times. We long for a different kind of community. One that doesn't simply tell us what to believe and how to behave but one that teaches us how to listen for the divine voice. We are looking for a spirituality not predefined but within which we can ask questions and learn from one another. My spiritual language and vocabulary are Christian, but I also believe that God is much bigger than my own vocabulary. I hope to continue learning from others who have experienced God in ways that I may not have words for yet.

Expanding Our Spirituality

This book represents my own journey to unform and re-form my soul. As an Asian American, I consciously and unconsciously hold Western values and ways of being. When I write about the Western context, I am referring to my experiences in the North American church, which has its own unique history and culture. I am also just as much Taiwanese and formed with the values and ways of being of my family. The reason I am not writing an "Asian American spirituality," however, is that I recognize that in order to expand my experience of God, I need to be formed by a diversity of voices, not just Asian.

In the past few years, I have sought resources and teachers in order to be formed by Black experiences of God, Latine experiences, Indigenous experiences, and a plethora of beautiful voices of color from around the world that reveal God to me. BIPOC communities have always expressed their spiritualities in subversive ways, but those spiritualities were not recognized. Although I am not qualified to write about these diverse spiritualities, this book reflects how my soul has been inspired and influenced by different authors of color. You will meet some of my inspirations along the way, interpreted through my Asian American female lens. I encourage you to explore their books listed in the Recommended Resources.

I use the term *BIPOC* intentionally to recognize that there are systemic injustices in the United States that disproportionately affect Black communities and Indigenous communities that may not be experienced by all people of color. As an Asian American, I hold more privilege in some spaces and circumstances than Black, Indigenous, or Latine communities. It is my responsibility to recognize the ways in which my privilege may harm the collective BIPOC community. I also benefit from the long history of activism led by Black, Indigenous, and Latine leaders as well as Asian Americans who risked their lives for the freedom I experience today. My work builds on theirs, and they continue to be my teachers.

I also write this book as a spiritual director and not a theologian. Although I will address ways that Western theologies, cultures, teachings, and traditions affect our faith, in the end, I am asking, How do these ideas affect our souls and our collective spiritual experience? Again, I refer you to other amazing authors who do the theological work of decolonizing our Christian faith tradition much better than I can.

I also want to recognize that sometimes, global churches hold even more rigidly than Western churches to the ways of spiritual discipline and formation that global pastors were taught in Western seminaries and by mission-aries. I believe that the root of this rigidity is still the West-ern church's historical hierarchy and patriarchy. The global church is sometimes unable to imagine that they can do things differently. In order to decenter Western the-ology as the primary authority, we need to intentionally free and empower global voices to reimagine spirituality and lead us as our spiritual teachers.

I assume that you are reading this book because you, too, have sensed that something is missing in the spiri-tual paradigms you grew up with, and you want to expand your experience of God. Perhaps you have a nagging and persistent question in your soul. Perhaps you've been going through the grueling process of deconstructing your theology—a part of the unforming work that makes us aware of who God is not, who the church is not, and who we are not. I find, however, that constant deconstruct-ing has left my soul with many questions. I am wondering, What's left? How do we participate with the Spirit in form-ing something new? My soul now needs the Creator God who speaks new things into being.

I present here a framework for reevaluating our spiritual formation paradigms and demonstrate how considering other cultural orientations can shift the way we experience a more diverse spirituality. I hope that this book opens the doors for further conversations about our cultural experi-ences so that we might share and expand our experiences of God together. Perhaps you and I will discover through this journey what our souls have been missing all along.

Our Spiritual Postures

This book is organized into three cultural orientations and nine postures. Through each orientation, I demonstrate how the formation journey shifts when we consider other cultural ways of being. The three orientations proposed in this book are from linear to cyclical, from cerebral to experienced, and from individual to collective. Each orientation is then followed by postures, ways we practically enter into the spiritual life. I use the word *postures* instead of *practices* because it emphasizes that the spiritual life is not a list of helpful activities to do but our ways of being in the world. Postures help us not withdraw from the real world but actually enter into all its complexities. Forming postures, however, takes time. So I include spiritual practices within each posture to help us strengthen our postures. For this book, I selected postures that have traditionally been absent from Western paradigms of formation: time, remembering, uncertainty, imagination, language, work/ rest, dependence, elders, and harmony.

Because in recent centuries the Western church developed in an individualistic culture, the focus of spiritual formation is often on the self, the inner life, and our personal growth. But we also have a *collective soul*. Our collective soul has a physical body called the church. What's often missing in spiritual formation paradigms is the health of our collective soul. Right now, as systemic injustices and white supremacy continue to oppress and traumatize BIPOC communities, our collective soul seems to be shriveling. Our approaches to spiritual formation need to form us as a community and for our communal presence in this world. Thus, we need an unforming and re-forming not just as individuals but also as a church. Unforming may mean collectively questioning what we've been taught and the way things are done. This communal unforming is not just with a critical spirit against the Western church, but we unform in order to reimagine and dream how we can experience community differently in diverse spaces. Thus, the third section of this book looks at a communal formation and not just an individual spiritual formation.

As you read through these orientations and postures, you may recognize that some ideas connect to themes also found in Western spiritual writings. If we are actively engaging the divine-human relationship, then the closer we draw to the divine, the closer we also draw to one another. The more we listen to and learn from one another, the more we will discover we share experiences of God. But the question at the heart of this book is, Why do we allow the Western traditions, rather than the non-Western cultures that have known these spiritual wisdoms all along, to be the authority? And what new insights can we gain when we start listening to non-Western perspectives?

I hope that white readers will engage the unforming journey by putting someone else's experience at the center. As an Asian American growing up in the United States, I am trained to put the white experience at the center. As I learned history and literature, the white experience was the center. As I watched TV and movies, the white experience was the center. As I work in predominately white institutions, the white experience is the center. As we consider other cultural orientations and postures not centered on the white experience, they may feel unfamiliar and awkward to us at first. The unforming and re-forming work for us all is to decenter whiteness in our experiences of God and to open up space in ourselves and in our communities for radically new experiences.

For people of color, these spiritual postures will likely feel familiar. We experience these postures in our homes and communities. But perhaps we have not named these postures as sacred experiences. I hope that people of color find comfort and rest here as these postures allow us to set-tle into our bodies and cultural ways of being and know-ing. We will discover that these cultural ways of being have always been our holy experiences of God.

For Reflection and Discussion

This book is incomplete until you add your own story and your family's story. So I offer questions at the end of each chapter for personal contemplation and to help you share your experiences in community.

1. In what ways have you felt a disconnect from the Western church?
2. If you think of your soul as the space where your most sacred self meets with God, what does your soul space feel like today? Do you have a clear view of yourself and God?
3. In what ways have you experienced unforming and re-forming in your spiritual life?
4. What areas in your life right now may need unforming? What areas in your life right now may need re-forming?

PART 1

Orientation → Cyclical

For much of my life, my experience of the spiritual life has been full of guilt and shame for not doing enough and not being enough. I feel guilty whenever I fall asleep while praying in bed and each time I glance at my dusty, unopened devotional books. As a woman, and especially as a woman of color, I have been taught that to become a good Christian, I need to serve sacrificially in the church. I have tried, but I often burnt out. When being a Christian is primarily measured by the amount of Scripture reading, prayer, and volunteering one does, I am a perpetual failure.

In the church, we tend to teach that formation occurs like this: a positive line of progression and growth.

But our experiences of the spiritual life often feel more like this: a messy and tangled web of confusion. At times, it seems unclear how we may be progressing or moving forward.

I propose here that neither of these images accurately reflects our spiritual lives. Instead, our formation is this: a cyclical movement into wholeness.

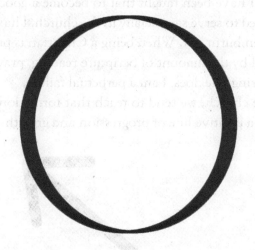

According to cultural psychologists Kaiping Peng, Julie Spencer-Rodgers, and Zhong Nian, the Western understanding of change tends to be linear.[1] Although change is unpredictable and disruptive, we in the West tend to believe that all change leads to progress. We are a future-orientated culture, so we expect change to result in continual advancement, just like the rising straight line shown in the first illustration.

In a study with white American and Chinese college students, cultural psychologists asked students to select a graph that best predicts their level of happiness as they age.[2] They found that the white American students were twice as likely to choose a graph with a linear progression. Although the students expected unhappy and happy moments in life, they also expected that over time, they would grow happier as they got older. Chinese college students, on the other hand, were more likely to select a nonlinear graph. They expected life to be a continual cyclical pattern from happy to unhappy, from unhappy to happy. They did not expect that age or time would bring a greater happiness.

An Eastern understanding of change tends to be cyclical. One of the earliest Chinese philosophers, Lao Tzu, thought of change not as a linear progression but as a circular pattern.[3] Whenever something positive happens and life gets better, then we can expect that something negative will happen and life will get worse. Whenever there's growth, it will be followed by a loss, and a loss is followed by growth. Daoist philosophy teaches us to accept and adapt to life as these constant cycles of change. These two different cultural orientations, then, lead to two different approaches to the spiritual life.

The Linear Journey in Western Formation

Since the Western church developed in a linear culture, we tend to teach faith and spirituality as a linear progression. We present faith as a step-by-step process of growth. We list the one, two, three discipleship steps that all Christians need to take. Even Western styles of preaching tend to be linear, often featuring a clear three-point sermon.

In Western spiritual writings, the image of a journey is often used to describe the Christian life, with a beginning, a destination, and markers of progress along the way. In the evangelical church, I was taught that faith begins with a decision followed by a prayer asking Jesus to come into my heart. The evangelical tradition identifies this moment as the beginning of a linear faith journey that also determines whether we will reach our destination: heaven. Oddly, I have never found that prayer in the Scriptures. Although I firmly believe that we can have life-changing and convicting encounters with God, I do not believe such experiences should be used to determine who's in or out of God's household. When I meet people who have said "the prayer" or claim "to be saved," I often don't find those qualifications to be accurate indicators of the health of their soul or their character as a human being. In the evangelical tradition, presenting faith as dependent on a single decision is dangerous because it does not adequately prepare us for a life of long faithfulness.

A linear orientation values progress, production, and perfection. If we believe our spiritual lives should continuously move upward, then that creates levels of achievement and a false expectation of perfection. We then need to produce results in order to demonstrate that we are growing. We strive for "Christ-likeness" but do so by putting on appearances of a perfect life instead of letting Jesus's compassion and utter love for messy people form us into Christ-likeness. Given an unattainable illusion of perfection, we set goals and expect formation to be productive by helping us improve ourselves. We then look to the current spiritual formation fad or engage the next new contemplative practice for self-improvement. We use spiritual practices as a way to make us feel accomplished as we check them off the list. We falsely expect that by putting in more effort—praying more, meditating more, or reading more Scripture—God will make life better and better, easier and easier. We also want our progress to be measurable, so we rely on moral dos and don'ts as measurements of holiness, or we expect to cultivate more virtues and rid ourselves of vices. Whenever we don't see progress or inner change as quickly as we expect, we get frustrated.

In Asian and Asian American churches, we are especially drawn to this achievement-oriented spiritual formation we've learned from Western churches. Asian pastors formed in Confucian patriarchy easily latch on to the power of assessing faith based on morals and achievements. Under a patriarchal system, male leaders of the church have the power to set the standards for progress in spiritual formation and to judge who is a good Christian and who is not. Just as Asian immigrant families futilely strive to prove that we are "American" by working hard and fitting in, as Christians, we can fall into the trap of trying to prove that we are "Christian." This meant that my earliest understanding of formation was filled with endless shame and admonitions that I was not measuring up. I frantically served in the church and in the community in order to make up for my insufficiencies. When spiritual maturity is measured against perfection, I get caught in a never-ending cycle of performance trying to meet the demands of a false perfection.

I still remember the words that began my unforming. An Asian American pastor and mentor, Dan, once said to me, "One day you'll make a big mistake, but the people around you will love you anyway. On that day, you'll be free, and you'll be able to more fully receive God's love for you." These words continue to resonate in my soul. They reveal to me how easily I can get caught up in the drive for flawless performance, even in spiritual things. The push for perfection in performance is not just a Western trait, but it has become the standard for modern culture, no matter where we are in the world.

The strength of a linear cultural orientation in spirituality is that it is optimistic, hopeful, and focused on growth. Even in suffering and grief, we can soothe our pain with the belief that God can use our sufferings for good. We expect positivity and growth even in the deepest of sufferings. The drawback of a linear orientation is when things don't go as planned, when life turns messy and complicated, we lack the spiritual vocabulary and depth needed to navigate. A linear spirituality is particularly insufficient for BIPOC communities because it cannot account for the perpetual cycles of oppression, violence, and injustice. Our linear expectations fail when no amount of reconciliation or redemption can make right or make better the atrocities of racism and white supremacy.

Circles

A cyclical orientation provides an alternative approach to the spiritual life. The image of a circle is found in many non-Western traditions. Cherokee theologian Randy Woodley explains that in many Native American cultures, the circle is used as a symbol of spirituality because it is the symbol of nature.[4] Creation reflects a cyclical, not linear, pattern of life—from the rotations of the earth and moon to the changing of seasons to blood circulating in our bodies. Indigenous communities learn to live in harmony with the cycles of nature. Farmers and gardeners also learn to understand the cyclical pattern of nature. But our modern spiritual practices often look more like a factory line for mass production rather than the natural cyclical patterns of life.

In a cyclical orientation to the spiritual life, there is no finish line. There are no steps or stages. Our spiritualities are simply our relationships with God; there is no point when it ends. Steven Charleston, an Episcopal priest and elder in the Choctaw Nation, writes, "It is all a circle, the ancestors said—an endless circle within a circle. The drum is a circle. The dance ground is a circle. The earth is a circle. There is no us or them, no top or bottom, no beginning or end, no lines of division—only a seamless embrace. The answer is within. It has existed since before time began, and it will be there long after the last campfire fades."[5] In Indigenous communities, a cyclical spirituality is reflected in the circles found in rituals and celebrations. Circles remind us that instead of being a destination to reach, the spiritual life is the transformation that is happening within as we experience the sacredness of God, the earth, community, and ourselves.

The circle is also found in East Asian spirituality represented by the yin-yang symbol. Within the circle are the continual cycles of change through which we experience the fullness of life. Korean theologian Chung Hyun Kyung writes, "The formation of a living spirituality is a continuous process of birth, death, and rebirth."[6] Although a cyclical spirituality is not optimistic, it is realistic as it reflects the movements of joy and grief as we learn to hold these cyclical experiences together.

In a cyclical spirituality, one in which there is no destination, we continuously return to where we began. Howard Thurman describes the spiritual life with the image of a
river, which has a cyclical ecosystem. He writes, "The goal
and the source of the river are the same!"[7] All water comes
from the sea and returns to the sea. In between, there are
times of flood and times of drought. He writes that in the
same way, "the source of life is God," and the movement of
the spiritual life is a returning to God.

I believe that in a cyclical formation, we are also returning to ourselves. We began not when we were born but
when God first imagined us. Our spiritual lives are the
cyclical journey of becoming that person God first saw, still
sees, and will always see in us. In a cyclical formation, we
are never incomplete or insufficient, but along the way, our
visions become distorted as we try to conform to the social
expectations around us. We may lose sight of who we truly
are. Through prayer, we connect to divine sight in order to
see ourselves again. Each time we return to God, our center, we are reminded of our sacred selves. On those days,
when I can no longer see myself clearly, I enter into the
space I share with God, and I ask, "God, when you first
imagined me, who did you see?"

Coming into Our Wholeness

When Mother Teresa was asked a question about the total
number of conversions she had brought about in her ministry, she redirected the question and responded, "I hope
I am in the process of conversion. I don't mean what you
think. I mean I hope we have converting hearts."[8] Mother
Teresa avoids tallying conversions as a sign of the success

or failure of her ministry. Instead, she humbly refers to her own formation, and in so doing, she invites us into the continuous cycles of conversion and change. Mother Teresa went through her own unforming as she experienced loneliness in ministry and wondered if God had abandoned her. Yet she continued her ministry because she believed her formation came from seeing Jesus in the face of every person she served. A cyclical formation can be frustrating, as we are continuously unforming and re-forming. Sometimes we feel like we're coming back to the same issues again and again—the same wounds, the same bondage. This is the work of unforming. Sometimes we are coming back to deep generational wounds that have been cycling through our family's story for centuries. But spirituality was never meant to be easy. In a cyclical orientation to formation, we see God is doing the work of transforming us. Of course that's hard! We are responsible for being present to the change and the work we need to do.

If our formation journeys are a continuous cycle of unforming and re-forming, then one way we can unform our linear expectations of perfection is by practicing making mistakes. For the past ten years, I've been continuously enrolled in some sort of art class. I've tried drawing, oil painting, watercolors, photography, whittling, and pottery. I'm not good at any of them. But I've come to think of my weekly art class as my weekly practice in failing. It's good for my soul to practice failing and for my hands to make big sloppy messes. Making mistakes is part of being human, and I am not any less worthy because of my mistakes. Some time ago, I began to realize that it's actually the imperfections that make a piece of visual art interesting and beautiful.

A cyclical paradigm presents us with a healing approach to our soul formation. Spiritual formation is not about progress but about wholeness. It values completeness over efficiency. It changes the way we relate to and interact with God. Cyclical formation offers no clear direction or measurable markers. The reason we may experience our spiritual formation as ups and downs, back and forth, highs and lows is not that we're lost or confused in the journey but that these are the natural cycles of the spiritual life. So even though I may experience the spiritual life like a tangled web,

I believe what God is working in me is actually an ever-expanding circle.

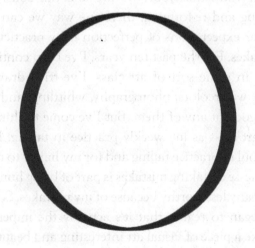

In wholeness, we experience ourselves more fully as our souls expand. As we transform, we create more room in our souls for ourselves, for God, and for others.

One professor explained to me a difference he noticed between his American students' and Asian international students' writing. Western writing usually follows a clear, linear outline with points A, B, and C. Again, this approach is also reflected in traditional sermons. In Eastern styles of writing, however, the student is not trying to make a linear claim of cause and effect or building an argument. Instead, the paper is used to reflect on or consider different perspectives of a central point. To American teachers, the Eastern way of writing can often feel like meandering thoughts and tangents, unless they can understand the difference demonstrated in illustrations 1 and 2.

Illustration 1: Western writing

    I.
        A.
        B.
    II.
        A.
        B.
    III.
        A.
        B.

Illustration 2: Eastern writing

The Eastern way of meaning making creates a cyclical pattern that revolves around one center. Repetition is used to expand an idea. When I listen to sermons in the African American tradition, I hear this same cyclical rhythm for filling out one main theme. Barbara Holmes writes in *Joy Unspeakable*, "In the black church, repetition is integral to the ministries of music and preaching. Rhythmic calls to worship invite congregants to ride repetitions to the inner sanctum."[9] Holmes argues that this rhythmic repetition enables a practice of communal listening that becomes a communal practice of contemplation when we experience the Spirit together. In the spiritual life, the cyclical movements of unforming and re-forming also draw us into a deeper experience of God and self.

While it is true that God's way of transformation in us is not the quickest and most efficient way of formation, we can trust that it is the most thorough and complete way to experience our wholeness. Although I may get frustrated that I don't see change or measurable progress, I have found that if I am present to God in the day-to-day, then when I look back, I can see how the space of my soul has expanded. A cyclical orientation invites us to experience God through alternative postures of time, remembering, and uncertainty.

For Reflection and Discussion

1. In what ways have you experienced a linear spirituality?
2. In what ways have you experienced a cyclical spirituality?
3. What is something you enjoy doing even if you aren't good at it? What are some lessons you have learned from practicing failing?
4. Take a moment to connect with God in your soul space. Ask God to show you who God imagined and created you to be. How are you becoming that person?

1

TIME

In the West, our understanding of time revolves around watches, calendars, and planners. On clock time, time only has one direction: forward. If time can only move forward, then we can "lose" time and become desperate to "save" time. We treat time like our own possession. We can see this whenever we become irritated and angry when we think someone is wasting *our* time.[1]

In our modern society, we never have to stop working because we can manipulate time by creating light at all hours of the day and night. Geographer Yi Fu Tuan writes of medieval cities, "The city began as an attempt to bring the order and majesty of heaven down to earth, and it proceeded from there by cutting itself from agricultural roots, civilizing winter, turning night into day, and disciplining the sensuous human body in the interest of developing the mind."[2] We invented our own technology to create 24–7 cities. Urban dwellers are conditioned to live by the rhythms of the city instead of the cycles of the earth. We created phenomena like "rush hour" and "overtime." Formed to live in perpetual hurry and to engage in nonstop activity, this notion of time values the instant.

This understanding of time as our possession, however, has always been an illusion. None of us actually owns time, and neither can we control time. Filipina theologian Melba Padilla Maggay writes that this particularly Western notion of time creates the illusion "that by sheer planning and management one can buttress oneself against the uncertainties of the future."[3] We plan as a way to calm our anxieties and to give us a sense of control over our busy lives. When we try to control time, time ends up controlling us. Our busy schedules take over our lives. This relationship with linear time forms us to be impatient, in a hurry, and constantly productive. This anxiety-ridden relationship with time has carried over into our spiritual lives. We tend to impatiently wait on God's responses to us based on our understanding of days, months, and years. We balk at the seemingly slow work of God.

God's Rhythm of Time

God seems to have a very different understanding of time. We see this in the Scriptures when God's promise to Abraham and Sarah that they will have descendants as numerous as the stars begins with one child, conceived when Abraham is one hundred years old and Sarah is ninety. Sarah, who struggled for so long with the pain of infertility, finds God's timing so painful she laughs. I imagine her laugh was a scornful one, not a lack of faith, as male theologians have traditionally interpreted. We also see God's sense of timing as the Israelites wander the desert for forty years and live in exile for seventy years. Through these stories, God doesn't seem to be in a hurry. Sometimes it even seems God is unaware of or even callous toward how much pain and suffering is experienced in the waiting. At the same time, these stories also show that God is not limited by the human invention of time and that God can move outside of time.

Those who grow up in cultures that place a high value on hospitality learn an alternative posture of time. They learn that an event or meeting begins not at the scheduled time but when all the guests have arrived. One moves from one meeting to another not because of a planner but when one conversation has naturally come to an end and a new one begins. Melba Padilla Maggay explains of Filipino time, "We do not start just because the clock says so, nor end just because it is 'time,' just like the Eskimos who laughed when they first heard a factory whistle in a salmon cannery. It seemed to them ridiculous that one should begin and stop work because of a factory whistle."[4] The movement of life determined by a rhythm of people instead of a clock seems much more in tune with God's sense of timing.

There are other understandings of time not measured by the Western calendar. Agricultural, lunar, and liturgical calendars follow seasons and other cycles. Some Asian cultures follow two calendars. They use the Western calendar for economic purposes and the lunar calendar for remembrances and celebrations. The lunar calendar guides us to live in harmony with the movements of the moon. Each celebration on the lunar calendar reminds me that my ancestors followed a different rhythm of time not determined by the colonial, economic power of the Western calendar.

Seasons give us a clue that there is an alternative approach to formation not measured by clock time. We don't often measure growth in plants and trees by time; instead,

we observe growth through the way plants transform
through the cycle of seasons. We may suddenly notice that
the flowers have bloomed or the leaves have turned red.
In the same way, our spiritual transformations happen in
seasons. We experience blooming and dormancy, growing
and dying, but we cannot control these cyclical changes.
We have to allow each change in us to come to fruition
regardless of how much time it may take.

In a cyclical spirituality, our interactions with God are
continuous. There's no point where we finish or complete
our formation, so there is no hurry to be done. We are not
"projects" to God. God is not in a hurry to be finished with
us. Therefore, we assess our formation not by how long it
takes but by the fullness of inner transformation. In the
spiritual life, we are attuned to whatever may be changing
in us through the cyclical seasons of life. Even if one season comes to an end, we then pay attention to the spiritual
movements of the next season.

A few years ago, in order to better live into God's sense
of time, I needed to reset my internal clock. A linear formation was so ingrained in me, I was doing everything out
of obligation. My mind and body consistently strived for
perfection and performance. So I stopped. I stopped all
praying, all Scripture reading, all commitments to serve or
lead in the church. I stopped taking steps to make progress in my life and get ahead. I unformed my sense of time
in order to experience God anew. As much as possible, I
stopped living with watches, clocks, planners, and calendars. Instead of noting hours and days, as much as possible, I lived by light and dark. Instead of marking weeks
and months, I observed the changing seasons around me.
I wanted my soul to long for the sacred. I wanted to desire
God for God's sake, not because I needed something from

God. So I committed to lingering with God rather than scheduling God into my busy calendar. I wanted my life to be led by desire and my soul's ache for more. So I committed to listen and respond to my desires. When I felt a desire to be in silence and prayer, I immediately stopped to listen. Whenever my soul was inspired by words, I stopped to hold and contemplate those words. When I desired to play, I stopped all else to have fun. I made commitments to serve or lead only when I felt the stirrings of the Holy Spirit or my own soul's excitement. The practice of responding immediately to my desires rather than routines trained me to be more attuned to my inner voice and the movements of the Spirit. I experienced a new freedom in a spirituality of desire rather than disciplines.

After a year in this spiritual reset, I found I actually spent more time in prayer, more time in silence and meditation, more time in the Scriptures, and more time in community because my soul longed for it. When we respond to our souls' desires for the sacred, we desire even more. When we respond to the Spirit, we hear the Spirit with more clarity because we learn to recognize what the Spirit's voice sounds like when she resonates within us. Of course, I still had to go to work and not be late to meetings, but even in my work, I found a greater patience and less anxiety about my performance. When I gave God unrestricted time, I could unform my impatience with how my life is progressing. Rather than constantly planning for the next big change, I found more contentment in the present.

Waiting

In order to live into God's sense of time, we must learn to embrace a posture of waiting. The Israelites waited in the desert and in exile. Wandering the desert, however, was never wasted time; it was formative time. In the desert, the Israelites experienced God in fire, God in water, God in food from the heavens. In exile, the Israelites experienced God while living as strangers, as migrants, and as neighbors in a new land. Something happens in the waiting. In the waiting, God shows up, or more accurately, we show up to God. In seasons of waiting, we become more attentive to the movements of the Spirit. Waiting often forces us to stop our constant activities and look to God. We learn in the waiting that God cares less about what we do or accomplish and more about the kind of person we are through any season of life. Rather than asking what's next, we can ask, How am I changing in this season? How am I experiencing God in the waiting?

Whenever I lead retreats or meet with my spiritual directees, I avoid using the term *spiritual disciplines.* When we think of disciplines, we think of actions that we need to schedule into our day or week. Disciplines require us to exercise our own willpower and self-control. Over time, we can engage with spiritual disciplines as routine and not even notice or pay attention to what we're doing. We might eventually forget or feel unmotivated to engage in spiritual disciplines and then feel guilty and blame ourselves for our lack of commitment. We can also lose our sense of the sacred when we think formation is about following routines and disciplines.

Instead of practicing disciplines, we need to re-form our spirituality to pay attention to our desires. Our desires can make seasons of waiting painful, because our yearnings for what's next can overwhelm us and take over all our thoughts and emotions. But instead of suppressing our desires, we need to listen to them. Under a patriarchal system, the church has taught us that our desires, particularly our sexual desires, are evil. But desires are part of our humanity. Our desires come out of our need to be seen, to be loved, and to live a life that is meaningful. Our desires are constantly stirring within our souls. When we ignore them, we ignore our sacred selves and the movements of the Spirit. Rather than viewing them as something to be ignored or suppressed, we need to learn to discern and pay attention to our desires. Our desires need to be part of our conversations with God even as we wait. Instead of focusing on spiritual disciplines, we can ask, What spiritual practices stir my desire to experience God?

Slow Reading

A practice I've found helpful to live into God's sense of time is the slow reading of Scripture and other sacred texts. You may have used a system like a Bible reading plan. Your goal was to read the whole Bible. You set a schedule and accomplished your task chapter by chapter. This is a linear way of engaging the Scriptures. But as we age, our relationships with the Scriptures can also evolve. We will be in the story of God for the rest of our lives. There is no hurry. Rather than reading a passage a day or trying to get through the Bible in a year, stay with one passage or section of Scripture for an extended period of time. Try reading the same passage every day, or return to the same passage every week instead of moving on. Read the words again and again. The purpose is no longer to finish or complete but to let the words linger in your soul. Let the words come to you throughout the day. Do not move on to another passage until the words form you or until the words change you. This means you may be meditating on the same passage for a month or even a full year. You are measuring not by the time it takes to read the words but by the transforming work the words are doing in you.

For Reflection and Discussion

1. How does your culture relate to time?
2. Think of a season in your life when you had to wait. How did you experience God in the waiting? How were you changed by the waiting?
3. What desires are stirring in you in this season of life? How are you experiencing God in those desires?

2

REMEMBERING

As members of a future-oriented culture, Americans too easily forget the past. Our future orientation has left us unable to fully reckon with history. Thus, by not truly facing the past, in the United States, we continue to pass on the generational cycles and repercussions of constant racial violence, murders, injustices, systemic inequalities, and divides. The healing work of unforming and re-forming requires a spiritual posture that enables us to look back and hold the past, no matter how difficult or shameful. Sometimes this means facing generational wounds and the unspoken stories in our families. Collectively, this means facing our colonial and racist history, both as a nation and as a church. Christians of color have to wrestle with the dissonance in their belief in a religion historically led by white people and acknowledge the many ways the Christian faith has been used to oppress BIPOC communities. These are systemic issues but also soul issues because the failure to reconcile our past distorts our collective soul.

I have been particularly influenced by the teachings of Black theologian and mystic Howard Thurman. Born in 1899, Thurman lived most of his life navigating a segregated United States as a pastor and professor. For a time,

he pastored one of the first racially integrated congregations in San Francisco. In his early life, Thurman had the
opportunity to travel to India to engage in dialogue with
the Indian leaders resisting British colonial rule. He found
that he needed to answer the question "How can you still be
a Christian in a religion that oppresses you?" Not only did
he need to figure out a response to his Indian friends, who
found Thurman's Christian faith incompatible with the racism in the American church, but he needed to work out the
dilemma in his own soul too. For Thurman, answering
the Indian leaders' question required him to figure out who
Jesus is not (unforming) and who he believed Jesus to be (re-
forming). Thurman wrote the book *Jesus and the Disinherited*
as a result of his conversations in India.[1] Thurman's journey
makes me wonder, "What is my soul's question?" How do
I reconcile my own family's faith in the Christian tradition
with the Western church's history of colonialism in Asia?

My grandparents were born and raised in Taiwan under
Japanese occupation. My paternal grandparents had the
opportunity to attend university in Japan. It was there that
my great uncles and grandparents met Western missionaries and, through those missionaries, the Christian faith.
Because my grandpa and grandma were both Christians,
the matchmaker brought them together. They raised our
family with a faithfulness and commitment to the church,
particularly the missionary's Presbyterian church, but I
don't think my grandparents ever fully understood what
Presbyterian means. Because my grandparents required us
to do so, our family spent every Sunday at a small Taiwanese immigrant church outside of Chicago. All the aunties
and uncles of the church became my family too. I recognize in my story a history of war, colonization, and immi-
gration and the influence of Western religion.

All BIPOC Christians have a complicated relationship with the history of the Christian faith, whether through the history of white patriarchy, colonization, and slavery or, in the case of Indigenous communities, genocide. But I was never taught in my formation how to confront this history and what it means for my own faith. White Christians, too, must acknowledge and wrestle with this history. Rather than dismissing our faith altogether because of the destructive, inhumane ways Christianity has been used, our work is to discover who God was to our ancestors in generations past. A cyclical formation requires that we reckon with the past in order to live into our present and future.

Returning to the Past

A past orientation offers a posture for entering into the spiritual life that is different from a future orientation. For past-oriented cultures, history hasn't ended yet. We're still living in it and through its many ramifications. We don't know yet the full effects of the past. Past-oriented cultures tend to see history as cyclical. They don't think of change as advancement, progress, and growth. Changes result from the natural cycles of the earth, time, and human life. Humans throughout history are not progressing but repeating the same historical patterns. What happened hundreds or thousands of years ago is still very much impacting who we are today.

In a study of American and Japanese history classrooms, sociologist Masako Ema Watanabe found that American teachers asked twice as many "why" questions as Japanese teachers, and Japanese teachers asked twice as many "how" questions as American teachers.[2] Western

culture tends to be analytic, which means we explain historical events in terms of direct cause and effect and spend
less time considering the contexts of the events.[3] Holistic
cultures, however, look at historical events in context and
spend more time in the past, considering a wide variety
of direct and indirect factors and relationships. Asking
"how" questions creates more space to consider the great
complexities of the past not as isolated events but as many
layers of events, individuals, communities, and actions
that all interconnect.

How would our spiritual lives change if we asked ourselves "how" instead of "why"? As a spiritual director, I was
trained to never ask "why" questions. "Why" can imply
blame or shame. I believe that asking "how" in our formation is a humble posture for facing our history and allowing
our history to inform how we live today. Listen to the difference between the question "Why did colonizers and missionaries suppress Indigenous expressions of spirituality?"
and "How did colonizers and missionaries suppress Indigenous expressions of spirituality?" Asking why centers those
in power and their motivations. Asking how considers the
actions of the colonizers and the ways those oppressed
were affected. Asking "how" in addition to "why" changes
the conversation. It furthers our dialogue to consider how
we may unform the harm done to those oppressed so they
might re-form what was lost from their spirituality.

A spiritual posture that embraces the past while holding the present and future can be found in the word *sankofa*
from the Akan tribe in Ghana. *Sankofa* means "it is not
taboo to go back and fetch what you forgot."[4] The spirit
of *sankofa* encourages the practice of seeking the wisdom of
the past to inform the present. In fact, to de-westernize and
decolonize our spirituality requires that we collectively go

back to confront our history and remember the lessons
we should have learned through the generations. In past-
oriented cultures, the past is valued as a container of deep
wisdom for the future. Past-oriented cultures are fluid, as
the past flows freely into the present and future.

One important spiritual practice for engaging the past
is to connect with the spirituality of our ancestors. Ancestral practices are family rituals that remember and honor
our ancestors. When Western missionaries entered foreign
lands, they often labeled any ancestral practices as evil and
idol worship simply because the traditions were foreign to
their own culture and spirituality. Converting to Christianity often meant being cut off from an active connection
to our ancestors. The Western missionaries were culturally
blind to the fact that the Bible has a rich spirituality of
ancestors that is passed through each generation.

The God of Your Ancestors

The first time Moses physically encountered God, it was
through a burning bush. In that encounter, we learn God's
name, *I AM WHO I AM* (Exod 3:14). But we often don't
notice the description that follows God's name in Exodus
verse 15: "God also said to Moses, 'Say to the Israelites,
"The Lord, the God of your fathers—the God of Abraham, the God of Isaac and the God of Jacob—has sent me
to you." This is my name forever, the name you shall call
me from generation to generation.'" In this passage, God's
name is both universal, *I AM WHO I AM*, and specific, *the
God of Abraham, Isaac, and Jacob*. For some of us, our ancestors passed down to us a spiritual tradition with the universal I AM; for others of us, our ancestors passed down to us

a relationship with the specific God of the Bible. The God of Abraham, Isaac, and Jacob reminded the Israelites that regardless of how many generations pass, they will recognize God as the God of their ancestors and that their relationship with God came from the interactions that their fathers and mothers, grandfathers and grandmothers had with God. Moses's faith began not with this encounter but with the love of his mother, Jochebed, who raised him as his nanny in the Egyptian palace. I believe his mother's spirituality allowed Moses to recognize the Israelites as his own people and the God of Abraham as his God too. This burning-bush encounter with God was also a cultural turning point for Moses. By heading back to lead his people, he was also accepting his own ethnicity.

In the NIV translation of the Old Testament, God is referred to as "the God of your ancestors" numerous times. The Israelites met the liberator God because they "cried out to the Lord, the God of our ancestors, and the Lord heard our voice and saw our misery, toil and oppression" (Deut 26:7). This prayer of desperation reminds me that in those seasons when the cruelty and injustices of this world seem incomprehensible and we wonder if God even exists, we can make one last desperate plea for help to the God of our ancestors. Rather than depending on our own faith, we can lean on the long tradition of those who had firsthand experiences with the liberating I AM. We can take comfort in their witness that God has a long memory. Deuteronomy 4:37 says, "Because he loved your ancestors and chose their descendants after them, he brought you out of Egypt by his Presence and his great strength." God follows through with a powerful act of liberation not because of the Israelites but because of God's deep love for Abraham generations earlier. I find reassurance in this idea that God's love for us covers an expanse beyond our lifetimes and that God still sees and remembers us even in our children and grandchildren.

In cyclical time, sometimes we wait on God for a lifetime, and sometimes we wait for generations. The Bible is not a book of abstract teachings, but the story of God is presented as God's continual interaction with families from one generation to the next. One generation is not enough to get to know God. God reveals Godself through many generations. Abraham's spirituality was about the generations to come. Jesus's spirituality began with the generations before. As we open up the first pages of the Gospels, Matthew tells us that Jesus's identity and story began forty-two generations earlier through both patriarchs and matriarchs. Even Paul in his testimony declares, "I worship the God of our ancestors as a follower of the Way" (Acts 24:14). His new faith in Jesus does not disconnect him from the faith of his ancestors.

A Spirituality of Ancestors

We need the wisdom of our ancestors as part of our everyday spiritual rhythms. To re-form our spirituality, we must let our ancestors speak. We must draw from the depths of their experiences and knowings of God. Rather than constantly moving on from the past, we need to embrace our generational experiences of God. God pleaded with the Israelites before they crossed the threshold into the promised land: "Remember, remember, remember! Remember how your ancestors were unjustly enslaved. Remember how your ancestors were liberated. Remember your time in the desert." Remembering is a spiritual posture. Unless we remember who God was to our ancestors, we will forget in the future who God is to us. We need practices that help us pay attention to the gentle nudges, dreams, and memories that may be our ancestors speaking. We need practices that help our bodies remember. We also need practices of story-telling so our grandchildren will remember.

In addition to its roots in the Christian tradition, my spirituality also comes from my maternal grandparents. Like most of the Taiwanese, their spirituality involves acknowledging our ancestors by lighting incense, offer-ing food on the altar, and praying through the body by bowing. (Sadly, these practices were interpreted by West-ern missionaries as idol worship rather than practices of paying respect to and remembering our ancestors.) We set up altars of food in order to share a meal with our ances-tors. We light incense in order to pray together. We pray for our ancestors as they pray for us. In Latin American regions, a vibrant Catholicism is filled with the sights and smells of candles and altars used to honor the saints who have gone before us. These ancestral practices are vibrant and engage the full body, including all our senses. We need ancestral practices to help us connect to our generational experiences of God.

Just as the Israelites were given holidays to help them remember their ancestors' journey with God, many non-Western cultures also set aside days for remembering our ancestors. Some Confucian-based cultures celebrate Tomb Sweeping Day, just as some Latin American cultures cel-ebrate Día de los Muertos. These days include practices of communal remembering. On Tomb Sweeping Day, we clean our ancestral tombs as families. These holidays are not solemn affairs like funerals or commercialized like Hal-loween; they are celebrations. The family gathers to be seen and visited by their ancestors. Indigenous spirituality particularly teaches us a posture of receiving the rich wisdom of our ancestors. Steven Charleston writes poetically of his ancestors in the Choctaw Nation in his book *Ladder to the Light:*

> Our eternal grandparents. They are watching over us, all those who have gone before. They are our ancestors, and they have seen enough in their own lives to know what we are going through. They have survived economic collapse, social unrest, political struggle, and great wars that raged for years. Now, from their place of peace, they seek to send their wisdom into our hearts, to guide us to reconciliation, to show us our mistakes before we make them. Their love for us is strong. Their faith in us is certain. When times get hard, sit quietly and open your spirit to the eternal grandparents, who are still a part of your spiritual world. Receive their blessing, for their light will lead you home.[5]

We must learn to actively listen for who God was to our ancestors in order to learn who God is to us today.

A spirituality of many generations recognizes that the spirits of our ancestors are still alive, active, and with us. For those who grew up without ancestral practices, you may have long been cut off from actively remembering and connecting with your history and traditions. It may be frustrating now to attempt to find the pieces. The generations before you may have already passed. Some of us may not know the stories of our ancestors because those stories were too painful to tell. Those who grew up in an abusive family may find that the past is hidden—or if revealed, traumatic. So we need to proceed in these spiritual practices with great care to attend to our souls and the souls of our families with compassion. For now, connecting with our ancestors may be slow and may occur only in pieces and fragments and small memories that we cherish. Still, we may take comfort in the truth that although we may not know our ancestors, our ancestors know us. Those of us who are disconnected from our ancestral homelands can be assured that our bodies still remember the lands our families are from.

In the Old Testament narratives, when someone's life on this earth comes to an end, the NIV translation often describes the death in this way: "Then David rested with his ancestors" (1 Kgs 2:10). I find this image comforting. It reminds me that as we leave some members of our families for a season, we are welcomed by other family. And with our families, we find rest. Our biblical ancestor Solomon blessed the congregation of Israel in this way: "May the Lord our God be with us as he was with our ancestors; may he never leave us nor forsake us" (1 Kgs 8:57).

For Reflection and Discussion

1. Describe the spirituality that was passed down to you.
2. In what ways has a Western history of colonialism, slavery, or genocide affected your family? How does this history affect your own faith?
3. In what ways are ancestors remembered and acknowledged in your culture?
4. What stories, wisdoms, or keepsakes have been passed down to you from your ancestors?

3

UNCERTAINTY

The ancient Greeks invented logic. They took pride in the agora, an open and public space where male citizens were free to exchange ideas and debate. This dynamic culture of debate influenced Western thinking and values. In Western education today, children continue to be trained on these same principles. In such a debate culture, the goal is to arrive at absolute truths, and contradictions are not logical. Cultural psychologist Richard Nisbett explains, "If one proposition was seen to be in a contradictory relation with another, then one of the propositions had to be rejected."[1] Tools such as categorizing and classifying are necessary in such a culture to define terms, make concepts clear, and create rules. Classifying has become one of the foundations of Western science. The defense of singular, one-dimensional ideas has evolved into our current polarized political culture.

The values of Greek philosophy influenced the growth of the Western church. The early theologians of the church prioritized what we believe and defended those beliefs by developing creeds, theologies, and written liturgies to convey the principles of the Christian faith. This process is necessary for the growth of a movement and reflects early church leaders' best attempts to live the Jesus way faith-fully, but it created a lopsided formation experience for the church. The result is a faith primarily centered around what we can know and figure out about God. We devel-oped theologies as a way to make God understandable and dependable. The need to clearly defend beliefs fractured the church into hundreds of denominations.

Western spirituality developed based on a desire for cer-tainty. A spirituality of certainty utilizes religion to give us a sense of control by setting rules and delineating beliefs that will not change. A spirituality of certainty is located in the mind. It is verbal and literate because it depends on human language to define God. Bible studies, written lit-urgies, prayer books, devotionals, and Sunday schools all come out of a formation meant to define and know God. Ultimately, we look for a God who is safe and predictable because we want our lives to be safe and predictable.

Those with privilege and power can especially build their lives around the delusion of certainty. Those with more influence and wealth can attempt to build up walls of protection against uncertainty by using their power to control circumstances and the people around them. But any certainty we attain is always temporary. Those who live in constant poverty and oppressive conditions recog-nize they have no choice but to live in a constant state of uncertainty. In his book *On Job*, liberation theologian Gustavo Gutiérrez wrestles with the privileged theology of the West, which does not address the injustices and suffer-ings endured by the innocent.[2] A spirituality of certainty cannot account for the suffering and tragedies that fall on both the deserving and undeserving alike. Triumphalism is the false assumption that we, the privileged, deserve to keep moving upward, to achieve, and to succeed. The US

culture of triumphalism allows us to pretend that because
we worked hard, good things come to us, and we are therefore also immune to bad things. Triumphalism has also
invaded how we live into our faith. A "just work harder"
society creates a "just work harder" religion. Because of
our privileged positions in life, we are surprised by suffering each time it comes near. Such a faith crumbles before
the suffering of the innocent.

A Spirituality of Suffering

Certainty is an illusion. Communities that learn to navigate life without power and privilege can teach us how to
live in constant uncertainty through the inevitable cycles
of suffering. There is a difference between a theology of suffering and a spirituality of suffering, however. A theology
of suffering asks why. A spirituality of suffering may not be
able to explain why but allows us to stay in the discomfort
of not knowing and not understanding to survive and to
be present to the suffering community. For communities
that live under systems of oppression, the spiritual life is
necessary for survival and not just to ensure the privilege
of rest and care. Spirituality cultivates the sustainability of
our souls and the sustainability of our bodies.

James Cone describes a spirituality of uncertainty
among those forced into slavery. He writes in *The Spirituals and the Blues*, "In order to understand the black slaves'
reaction to their enslavement, it is necessary to point out
that their reflections on the problem of suffering were not
'rational' in the classical Greek sense, with its emphasis
on abstract and universal distinctions between good and
evil, justice and injustice. The black slaves had little time

for reading books or sitting in the cool of the day, thinking about neat philosophical answers to the problem of
evil."[3] Instead, those in slavery experienced evil and suffering through what was done to their bodies. Evil was not
a philosophical matter but personified in the slave own-
ers. Their spirituality, then, was not rooted in an effort
to understand suffering but grew out of a desire to experience a God who is present to our suffering. Cone argues
that with their bodies, they cried out to this God through
singing spirituals. He writes, "Instead of testing God, they
ritualized God in song and sermon. That was what the
spirituals were all about—a ritualization of God in song.
They are not documents for philosophy; they are material
for worship and praise to the One who had continued to
be present with black humanity despite European insan-
ity."[4] Slavery was so senseless and dehumanizing that no
amount of reasoning could provide comfort or certainty.
Instead, those in slavery needed embodied and collective
spiritual practices to survive.

   In her book *Joy Unspeakable*, womanist theologian
Barbara Holmes writes about the moan as the only fitting
response of the soul to the deep pain and disorientation
experienced by the Africans taken into captivity. She
writes, "The only sound that would carry Africans over the
bitter waters was the moan. Moans flowed through each
wracked body and drew each soul toward the center of
contemplation."[5] Holmes explains that the moan was the
only fitting sound of prayer shared by those on slave ships
who did not speak the same languages but shared the same
cry of distress. The moan became their united sound of a
desperate prayer. These moans and the cyclical rhythms of
spirituals sustained the soul in times of uncertainty when
what was happening all around could not be explained or

justified with words. Although we cannot fathom or relate
to the atrocities experienced by those in slavery, their songs
and stories show us that every human being knows deep
within their inherent dignity and worth; therefore, those
in slavery believed in a God who also saw their dignity as
human beings. We need a spirituality that enables us to
access that dignity through all circumstances.

Sustainable Spirituality

Those educated in the West may have difficulty imagining that there could be an alternative to the rationalism
of Greek philosophy, but other ancient cultures did not
begin with the premise that logic is the only way to think
about the world. The ancient Chinese, for example, didn't
care much about logic; they were more concerned with
harmony. Chinese philosophers had a different starting
point and thus a different end—quite different from Western philosophy. Some of the founding principles of Daoist
philosophy include change, contradiction, nonaction, and
harmony.[6] Daoists believe that the only absolute truth is
change. The assumption of constant change rather than
unchanging rules forms us to expect uncertainty. Further-
more, rather than assuming absolute truths exist, Daoists
believe that contradictions naturally exist in all things.
For example, we cannot understand good unless we also
understand evil. Thus, contradictions are always to be
held together, not separated. Being formed in contradictions rather than dualisms forms us to hold uncertainty
without needing to have resolution. We need contradictions to experience the fullness of life and to experience
the fullness of God. In the spiritual life, if we hold the

paradoxes and contradictions of God, we can also hold the mysteries and vastness of God.

Finally, in relation to nature, Daoists believe in nonaction. Nonaction is the principle of adapting to the movements and changes of the environment. Nonaction is very different from the foundations of Western colonization and our modern economy, which operate out of the false belief that the role of humanity is to master and control the environment. This sense of control over creation leads to trying to control other people and even God. Nonaction does not mean not doing anything; instead, it means we recognize the changes that are beyond our control or don't need to be controlled.[7] A posture of nonaction also frees us from greed and utilizing creation or other people for our own benefit. It is the opposite of conquest.

Although I long for the comfort of certainty as much as anybody else, I think we need a spirituality that forms us for uncertainty. I love liturgy, and I recite liturgical prayers daily. Western hymns are also beautiful descriptions of our Western faith that provide certainty. But I recognize that while the comfort and strength of written liturgy and hymns give us words of certainty whenever we feel uncertain, we fail to learn a spiritual posture that helps us stay in the uncertainties of life without having to define, give words to, comfort, or justify our experiences. We have done the same with our practice of prayer, as we tend to fill our prayers with the comfort of our own words instead of waiting in the uncomfortable space of silence and listening. We are uncomfortable in the long silences that the unexplainable circumstances of life create. We try to explain and defend on behalf of God.

A faith that tries to define and defend God, however, can lead to false assumptions that we can somehow control God. We then tend to blame God when we've lost control and certainty. Miguel De La Torre writes, "But don't we make a mockery of God when we create a theology designed to save God from God instead of doubting God's presence and goodness? A relationship that fails to yell and scream and curse a God for ungodly acts is a faith in denial."[8] God doesn't need us to defend God. A spirituality of uncertainty is one that wrestles, questions, and doubts God instead of trying to cover over or move on with certainty.

A posture of uncertainty is a recognition of how much we don't know about God. Seventeenth-century Mexican poet Sor Juana writes in one of her ballads, "Oh if there were only a school or seminary where they taught classes in how not to know as they teach classes in knowing."[9] Our Western theological institutions train leaders to be experts on knowledge so that even our leaders are not prepared for the unexpected changes and tragedies in the communities they lead. This reliance on knowledge for certainty is true in all cultures where the privilege of education allows us to look to our own abilities to find certainty. In his studies of Chinese religions, geographer Yi Fu Tuan observes that the Chinese nobility focused their spiritual practices on the study of astronomy and the design of temples, palaces, and cities.[10] He writes, "The elite believe that they can impose a certain order on reality." People with power and education can use their religion to reinforce their power and give them a sense of control. Tuan writes, "In contrast, ordinary people, with less power to regulate their own lives, see reality as made up of largely arbitrary forces." Ordinary people practice spirituality in everyday places like a garden, beneath a tree, or alongside water as evidence that the supernatural could be found in ordinary places. Rather than establishing spiritual practices that involve the study of unseen and untouchable forces, their spiritual practices rest in places they can touch every day as they recognize all the ongoing life circumstances that are beyond their control. They look for the supernatural in everyday things because they need a power that comes from outside themselves to survive through all the unknowns of life. In the same way, we often study our faith like the Chinese nobility, looking for theories that justify our attempts to control life circumstances. But in the end, we all experience uncertainty, so we all practice spirituality like any ordinary folk—with rituals, practices, and symbols that help us find the sacred in life among the things we can't understand or control.

Uncertainty often begins in the body. It starts with dislocation, pain, sickness, hunger, violence, loss. If uncertainty is first experienced in our bodies, then a spirituality of uncertainty is also found through our bodies. Not knowing removes the focus from the mind, where anxiety is located, and moves us into our bodies. We need spiritual practices that do not rely on words but allow us to engage our bodies. When my mind is filled with stress or worries, I often engage in an extended spiritual practice like exploring the city, going on a long bike ride, or engaging an art project where I can "think" in colors, shapes, and textures instead of words. Constant repetitive motions help clear out my anxious thoughts and help me experience my body through the rhythms of movement.

We cannot ignore uncertainty. We live in it. Rather than ignoring the anxieties and tensions we may feel, we need to pay attention to them even if there is no solution. We unform the need for neat resolutions and happy endings. We unform the need to fix problems. We acknowledge the unsettled feelings, uncertainties, or unresolved issues in our lives. We become aware of the ways we're planning or organizing to give ourselves a sense of certainty and safety. As tensions arise, we acknowledge the holy wisdom of our body, mind, and soul as she communicates to us that something is not right. But rather than attempting to quickly resolve these issues and move on, we take extended time in our prayers to remain in the tensions. Healing comes from acknowledging the tensions rather than stuffing them down, covering them over, or becoming numb. We allow the discontent, disillusionment, fears, longings, and uncertainties to be our prayers. In uncertainty, we are attentive to our needs. We are also attentive to how the Spirit may be moving through the unknown and unseen. When we let go of the need to know and control, we give the Spirit the space to move.

For Reflection and Discussion

1. How do you respond to uncertainty?
2. How does your culture or family respond to uncertainty?
3. What rhythmic and embodied practices do you enjoy?
4. What uncertainties are you holding right now? How are you responding to these uncertainties?

PART 2

Orientation ⇄ Experience

When Western missionaries entered foreign lands, they encountered the many creative, vibrant, and diverse ways that human cultures interacted with the divine and supernatural. They experienced different smells and tastes, ways of using the body, and textures, sounds, and colors. Instead of being inspired by the beauty of diversity, however, they responded with fear, domination, and control. Theologian Cláudio Carvalhaes writes in *Liturgy in Postcolonial Perspectives* that the agenda of colonialism was to eradicate differences and control differences with a Western uniformity.[1] For the Western church, conversion was achieved not just through teaching a standard set of beliefs but through controlling bodies and sensory experiences and thus suppressing the communal spirit of a culture. Sociologist Giuseppe Giordan writes, "The control that religion has exercised over the body has been implemented through a complex system of rules, rules governing everything from sexuality to dreams, from food to desire, from work to emotions, from medicine to dress, from birth until death, including even the celebration of mourning."[2] I weep when I think of all that has been lost because our religion has controlled and suppressed our bodies.

As white voices became the authority for who God is and what the Christian life should look like, we lost the ability to experience God for ourselves. The way we engage our faith with our bodies often looks, smells, sounds, tastes, and feels Western. I am saddened every time I visit churches in Asia that look and feel exactly like any church I can walk into in the American suburbs. As soon as I step out of the church, I notice a stark contrast between the standardized culture inside the church and the local culture outside of the church. I can feel the foreignness of Christianity. To unform our spirituality, we need to experience God in our bodies in ways that the white experience of God is not at the center of our spirituality.

In addition, the Western church has tried to limit spirituality to the mind by suppressing or neglecting the body. Western Christianity starts with the premise that forming right beliefs will lead to right practices, right morals, and a right society. Randy Woodley writes of these belief statements, "Euro-western civilizations always ask, 'What does the law say?' 'What does the constitution say?' 'What does the Bible say?' These propositional concerns are everyday topics for many Euro-Americans. The written word is given permission to override the heart and conscience of people on almost every occasion."[3] In this cerebral faith, "spiritual formation" often becomes a process of learning these right beliefs through study and then living out what is studied through self-will and discipline. Spirituality, however, is lost in a cerebral faith because we no longer tangibly interact with a living and dynamic God. In a cerebral faith, God becomes an abstract idea. God becomes entirely invisible and unseen.

A non-Western spirituality begins not with the mind or belief statements but with experience. In a non-Western spirituality, experience is also a form of knowing. Experience is how we encounter God. Different ways of knowing lead to different approaches to spiritual formation. Woodley explains that in Native American religions, faith is learned through practice rather than beliefs. An experienced spirituality begins with freeing our bodies, emotions, and practices as our ways to know God. Howard Thurman wrote of experience: "When this experience becomes an object of thought and reflection it is then that my mind creates dogmas, creeds and doctrines. These are the creations of my mind and are therefore always *after* the fact of the religious experience. But they are always out of date. The religious experience is always current, always fresh. In it I hear His Voice in my own tongue and in accordance with the grain in my own wood. In that glorious and transcendent moment, it may easily seem to me that all there is, is God."[4] In experience, God is active. Therefore, an experienced spirituality opens us to be surprised by the expanse and the nearness of God and allows God to move and speak. We might encounter God through dreams and visions. We can expect to feel God tangibly even if we don't have words for what we may be experiencing.

The Spirit in Spiritual Formation

Through the Enlightenment, the West largely dismissed tangible experiences of the Holy Spirit because they couldn't be explained using science. In an experienced spirituality, body and spirit become united again because they were never meant to be separated. Our physical experiences of God are supernatural, and our mystical experiences are just as physical. Theologian Simon Chan argues that most non-Western cultures are highly attuned to the supernatural movements of the spiritual realm in everyday life. The

spiritual realm includes the active presence of spirits, ancestors, and the Holy Spirit. Chan calls this awareness of the
spiritual in all things a "sacramental consciousness."[5] In a
sacramental spirituality, the material and spiritual are inter-
twined, and we can experience the supernatural through
our senses and practices. We are not trying to understand
God but to experience God. In a sacramental consciousness, our cultural traditions are fully infused with the spiritual, and the Holy Spirit is embodied in our movements,
expressions, and practices. The first step to unform and
re-form the loss of spiritual experiences in our bodies is to
connect with our sacramental consciousness once again.
We need to make the holy and sacred alive and embodied. We need to see and experience everywhere the mysteri-
ous, supernatural miracles of life.

Mujerista theologian Ada María Isasi-Díaz provides an
example of a sacramental spirituality in her book *Mujerista Theology*. She describes the altars she has witnessed
in the homes of many Latin American Catholic women:
"Our home altars are full of statues and are a tangible way
of making the divine present. It is at home altars that
God's presence is invoked, where mutual commitment and
responsibility between us and God are established. Our
home altars clearly indicate for us the divine is directly
accessible; that we do not have to depend on priests or pastors to relate to the divine."[6] A tactile spirituality gives the
powerless the power to connect directly with God because
they can access God in their own homes and through their
own bodies. For BIPOC Christians, these bodily connections to our cultures are essential for unforming our colonized bodies and re-forming our bodies as the central
location where we encounter God.

A sacramental consciousness is the center of an embodied spirituality. We need to wholeheartedly believe that our bodies are sacred and filled with the Spirit. Although we may be aware that we need to take good care of our bodies through healthy eating, exercise, and rest, those healthy practices are not yet infused with a sacred awareness until we can see the holiness of our bodies. Our bodies are the sacred sites that mediate our direct connections to God. We are equipped in our bodies to touch God, hear God, smell God, taste God, and see God, but we will encounter God only if we are expecting God to be right here. We need to redefine spiritual formation not as growing or learning, which can be centered on the mind, but as our dynamic and tangible everyday encounters with and in the Spirit.

I believe the Pentecostal tradition is the fastest-growing Christian tradition in non-Western parts of the world because it begins with experience. Pentecostal spirituality encourages us to see the supernatural everywhere. Non-Western peoples throughout the world have always held this awareness of the supernatural; thus, Pentecostal spirituality is natural to their way of being. They expect God to show up in dreams, visions, miracles, and prophecies. Carvalhaes writes, "Pentecostal Christians gained a somewhat immediate relation to God who manifested Godself in their own bodies with a different imprimatur of authenticity."[7] The Holy Spirit empowers the powerless by entering their bodies. In a Pentecostal spirituality, our emotional responses and physical reactions to the Holy Spirit are all ways we physically experience God. A Western education is not required for knowing God; instead, the Holy Spirit gives everyone the authority to know God through experience.

Hidden even within Western church history are the teachings of the Christian mystics who claimed to have supernatural encounters with God through visions or other miraculous occurrences. Teresa of Avila, John of the Cross, Francis of Assisi, and Julian of Norwich are just a few of the spiritual leaders who experienced a supernatural God. Their lives and teachings, however, have been overlooked and even dismissed by the church as if tangible experiences of God are abnormal and heretical. As I studied the mystics, I was surprised to discover that the mystical writings from centuries ago and the Pentecostal community today share the same vocabulary. Their descriptions of their visions and experiences of union with God are very similar. The Christian mystics were the Pentecostals of their time, and Pentecostals are the mystics of our time.

Many of us today believe in a supernatural God, but we may not have ever experienced a supernatural God. We practice spiritual formation without the Spirit. We need to learn how to bring our physical and spiritual worlds together as one integrated experience of the holy. We need to embrace our everyday, physical experiences as sacred and magical. Thus, our bodies are essential to our formation, because it is through our bodies that we interact with God.

Tactile Spirituality

In the late 1800s, a major shift occurred in how humans perceived their own bodies.[8] In that century, mirrors gradually became common household objects, and photography was invented. It became common for the wealthy to have their portraits taken. Our perspectives gradually shifted from experiencing our bodies based on what we feel to understanding our bodies based on what we see. Cultural historian Constance Classen writes that lighting, mirrors, and portrait photography "heightened consciousness of the visible body as compared to the felt body."[9] Human societies further amplified the body as a primarily visual object judged by appearances. The development of digital photography and social media in the last century has only exacerbated this phenomenon. Treating the body as a visual object further distorts our perceptions of beauty and of one another, and as Isabel Wilkerson explains in her book *Caste*, it allows the social construction of race and color to be used as a hierarchical system that elevates whiteness.[10] The work of unforming is the difficult task of undoing this disturbed way of seeing one another as objects. The work of re-forming is a journey of experiencing our felt bodies. To de-westernize our spiritual formation, we need to reclaim and rediscover our dances, expressions of joy and laughter, sharing meals, working, taking care of one another, and mourning as spiritual practices. We need kinesthetic and tactile spiritual practices that help us move into our felt bodies.

BIPOC communities have tried to fit our interactions with God into Western spaces with Western cultural norms, and within those spaces, we try to awkwardly readjust ourselves, find where we belong, and get permission to redecorate in order to fit our non-Western ways into the Western parameters of the church. The work ahead to unform our spirituality, however, requires that we break free from these Western parameters. Sometimes this task is referred to as "contextualization." Contextualizing, however, still assumes that the Western way is the standard way, and all

other ways are creative deviations. The work of unforming
and re-forming our souls is *not* contextualization. We are
not taking Western norms and adding ethnic expressions.
We are going back to what the missionaries should have
done in the first place, to allow our experiences of God
to be fundamentally changed by sitting and learning from
one another. Carvalhaes writes that historically colonized
communities still find subversive and creative ways to
reimagine worship and liturgy, and we need to learn from
these expressions. He writes, "While empires and colonization processes tried to fix rituals as a way of controlling
senses, understandings, and bodies, colonized people have
always intervened in these processes, creating, rebelling,
challenging, undoing, and redoing."[11] These practices are
ways in which colonized people have tried to break free
from Western-controlled spaces. Carvalhaes states that
we can reclaim our spiritual practices through other forms
of knowing, such as attending to our bodily movements,
senses, and emotions as expressions of our spirituality.

In the Scriptures, the presence of God is not abstract.
Our interactions with God are located on land, in places,
in bodies, in practices. This is why our cultural traditions,
stories, histories, celebrations, and rituals matter. They
form us as physical human beings. They help us connect
to the tangible presence of God through movements, art,
and storytelling. We need a re-forming of spirituality that
is not just based on homogeneous images, smells, objects,
and sounds predetermined by the Western church. We are
diverse not just in philosophy and thinking but in tastes,
odors, sounds, images, and textures. A vibrant spirituality incorporates body and place as we fully experience the
divine Spirit. The next chapters help us immerse ourselves

in a spirituality we experience through the spiritual postures of imagination, language, and work/rest.

For Reflection and Discussion

1. In what ways has your body been suppressed and
   controlled in your experiences in the church?
2. What sense experiences in your culture do you
   find sacred?
3. How did your family tangibly experience the
   Spirit? In your culture, what practices help you see,
   touch, smell, hear, and taste God?
4. How have you experienced God through dreams,
   visions, or other supernatural occurrences?
5. Do you primarily experience your body as seen or
   felt? How can you experience your body kinesthet-
   ically and tactually rather than visually?

IMAGINATION

For a few years, I served at a church in Taiwan. On the Sundays when it was my turn to prepare the elements for communion, I bought the foreign grape juice that was dark red in color rather than the local grape juice made with green grapes. Looking back, I realized I never questioned why I chose to buy the imported, harder-to-find, more expensive grape juice. A Western liturgical way was so ingrained in my body and imagination that I could not see the Eucharist beyond red grape juice. As Western leaders set the norms of our faith, they also suppressed our spiritual imaginations. Theologian Willie Jennings writes that Western colonialism and power created a "diseased social imagination."[1] It hasn't occurred to us that spirituality or community or God could look different from the dominant cultural expression of them. Thus, to embrace an embodied and experienced spirituality requires that we learn how to imagine once again and to imagine God anew.

Before we can imagine, however, we first need to unform our imaginations. Imagination is what led colonizers to fear and hate "the other"; they let their imaginations see the worst. In our modern world, we continue to perpetuate white superiority and white standards, which inhibit our ability to imagine beyond Western domination. For a season, I taught English to university students in Beijing. At the beginning of every semester, I had to prepare myself for the disappointment of my students. The students were told they would have a foreign teacher from the United States and a native English speaker. On the first day of classes, I walked into the large lecture halls, and as I made my way straight to the podium, I could always hear the room go silent. And the moment I introduced myself as their English teacher, I could see the faces drop on every student in the room. Their imaginations told them that a foreign English teacher must be white. Their imaginations told them that someone not white, someone who looked like them, would be an inferior teacher. I then spent the remainder of that class and the rest of the semester teaching with extra energy and excellence to prove that I could teach just as well. The distorted image of white as superior is a global phenomenon.

Those who had power in the Christian church created a God just like them—a white, masculine God. Our imaginations have been co-opted by those in power. Social psychologist and theologian Christena Cleveland writes in her book God Is a Black Woman, "Imagination is theology; we can only believe what we can imagine. And our cultural landscape hasn't given us many tools to imagine a non-white, non-male God."[2] In her work, Cleveland encourages us to utilize new images and spiritual practices to help us see God. We need to re-form imagination to challenge and thwart the historical white imagination. Rarely do we intentionally use our human capacity to imagine in our spiritual lives. We don't often allow our souls to wander and freely daydream. But we desperately need the powerful practice of imagination—a new way of seeing—to create a new way of being and experiencing. Imagination helps us see beyond our current reality of racism and white supremacy and envision a different way of community.

BIPOC communities may avoid imagination because we don't want to be disappointed by a false hope. We have been disappointed and disillusioned so many times in our continual experiences of racism that a spiritual posture of imagination cannot be based on an empty hope. Theologian Miguel De La Torre writes in his book *Embracing Hopelessness* that hope is a privilege not afforded to all in BIPOC communities. He says, "But for so many from minoritized communities where surviving into adulthood is itself a challenge, and where skin pigmentation ensures lack of opportunities to wealth and health, hope runs in short supply."[3] Whereas privileged communities might find hope in imagining a heaven where there will be no more racism, poverty, or tears, that vision dismisses the pain of reality right now. De La Torre writes that hope allows the privileged to be complacent and maintain the status quo by telling the oppressed to just wait.[4] A theoretical hope of unity is not enough to change our society or our churches. De La Torre argues that to truly address our deeply rooted systemic injustices, we need hopelessness and desperation to stir us into action. So the spiritual posture of imagining is not based on hope. To imagine, we must be discontent and angry at systemic injustices rather than hopeful. We imagine because we acknowledge our oppressive and unjust realities, and only the power of imagination will lead us to respond with creative and radical change outside of continuously racist systems. White superiority is so ingrained in our systemic and cultural ways of being that we need imagination to step into a new way of being that we have never experienced before.

The discontent of BIPOC communities motivates us to demand more of God and to want better for our families and communities. Walter Brueggemann assigns the practice of imagination to the work of a prophet, and in his book *The Prophetic Imagination*, he calls artists the modern-day prophets of society.[5] Artists are not afraid to imagine what may seem impossible. Brueggemann writes, "Thus every totalitarian regime is frightened of the artist. It is the vocation of the prophet to keep alive the ministry of imagination, to keep on conjuring and proposing futures alternative to the single one the king wants to urge as the only thinkable one." Artists can threaten the controlling narrative of those in power. Artists reside at the borders of our broken realities and their imaginations of a different possibility. In that in-between space, they express through color, sound, texture, movement, and word what doesn't yet exist. Artists can change the way we use words and help us hear and speak differently. Artists can help us change the way we imagine and show us an alternative reality. Imagination is the audacity to want, desire, and demand better—to break through the boundaries of cultural standards and norms, to experiment, and to express something new. I see imagination as the central posture to re-forming our collective soul.

Imagination as Prayer

Maybe it's been so long since you've imagined that you've forgotten how. Imagination is a powerful tool that can harm or empower. Imagining the worst possibilities can lead us down the path to anxiety or debilitating fear. If we lose the ability to imagine altogether, that can lead us to despair.

When we daydream, we are actively using our imaginations to work out something in our minds that might not have happened yet. We try to envision in our minds different outcomes. Young children can spend a long time playing pretend and imagining themselves in all sorts of roles. They can become superheroes, chefs, or teachers. But somewhere along the way, reality steals our imaginations. We become limited by what is practical. We become restricted by what's in front of us. We can no longer see or operate outside of our oppressive social, systemic, and religious structures. Just as we wouldn't reprimand a child for playing pretend, we need to free our imaginations from our own self-criticism.

God also needed to imagine in order to create. Thus, imagining is a holy act. Before speaking into being, God first had to see something that never existed before. Imagination is an active prayer in which the Spirit gives us the power of divine sight to see things anew, to see what we may have missed, and to see what might not yet exist. In our imaginings, we trust the Spirit to move and speak to us. The Spirit inspires. The Spirit is active. The Spirit expands our capacity to imagine. We imagine in images, colors, dreams, and memories, not just in words. Imagining is not wasted time. Rather, our souls imagine our deepest prayers, our holy discontents with reality, and our cries for what seems impossible.

In spiritual direction, whenever I sit with BIPOC and LGBTQI+ directees, we spend much of our time together in lament, anger, grief, and frustration. We lament each unjust loss of life that we see in the news or experience in our own communities. We rage at the systems that keep us in bondage. We grieve who we could have been if social expectations did not confine our individual and communal expressions of identity. We're frustrated, although not surprised, every time we encounter white privilege. We may spend months or even years together acknowledging, calling out, and expressing our lament, anger, grief, hopelessness, and weariness. We fully acknowledge the reality of our current circumstances without dismissing the pain or harm. But then at some point, our conversations slowly and carefully move toward imagination.

I ask my directees to remember their childhood and the moments when they were carefree and fully delighted in themselves. As they remember their past, I then ask them to imagine themselves today as that child and how they would be if our society and religious structures did not determine who they should be. Through imagination, we get a sense of what this world would feel like if it were made right. We need to be able to see and feel what is right and loving to live into it. For BIPOC communities, imagining practices helps us unform a white-centered perspective and posture in order to re-center our own stories. None of us have experienced the justice we long for. So how do we know what we're working toward? We don't know yet what Christianity looks like without its colonial and patriarchal baggage. So we need the powerful posture of imagination to see something that doesn't yet exist. In imagining, we trust our creativity. We imagine the society we want to live in and the community we want to be a part of. We imagine how our families and children would be if they could live in a world without systemic barriers. Imagination is refusing to let the "buts" and "impossibles" get in the way. Only the things we can first imagine are possible—if not in this generation then for the next.

Practicing Imagination

For those who have lost their imaginations, I offer the following practices to help stir our creativity again.

LISTENING TO THE NOISE

Before we can imagine, we must address the oppressive internal voices that restrict our imaginations. Most spiritual formation resources emphasize the practices of keeping silent or letting our thoughts go, but we also need spiritual practices for listening to the noise. Often, when we first begin to quiet down, intending to pray, the first thing that happens is all our inner voices come flooding in, and our to-do lists take over our soul spaces. As soon as we try to listen and imagine, the voices of reality flood in. External and internal voices enter our imaginations with worries, warnings, and practicalities. I often hear people complain that because of these loud internal voices, "I can't practice silence" or "I can't hear God." In our busy lives, we rarely stop to listen to our thoughts or emotions. We may notice them, but because we're in a hurry, we will quickly move on. So of course, as soon as we stop and become quiet, our mind says, "Finally! You are listening," and all our stored-up thoughts and emotions come rushing in. Therefore, we need a regular rhythm of stopping to fully listen to ourselves.

BIPOC communities, who may spend all day navigating white patriarchal spaces where our voices are not heard or are constantly questioned, have been trained to ignore or distrust our internal voices. The practice of listening to ourselves is a reminder that we are worthy of being listened to. In this practice, we make time to listen to how our thoughts, emotions, and bodies are communicating to us. We don't need to push away our thoughts. We don't need to ignore or move on. We've been doing that all day, so now we can take the time to listen—to attend to all our voices so we can free ourselves to imagine.

Those who have trouble accessing and recognizing their own voice especially need this practice. We need to listen to the surface-level thoughts, reminders, and to-do lists no matter how seemingly insignificant. By listening to all the reminders and warnings and giving them attention, we are letting our internal voices know that our needs and concerns are important. As we practice listening to the noise, all the surface-level voices will slowly move on as they are heard, and we can begin to access the voices that are buried deep within us. Through this practice, we will slowly begin to distinguish our own voices from others. Women especially have mixed into their internal noise the voices of patriarchy. Recognizing our own voices and wisdom may at first feel unnatural. Only when we can access our own voices are we liberated to then freely dream and imagine something new.

Dreaming

Another practice I have found helpful for reconnecting to my imagination is paying attention to my dreams. I barely remember my dreams, so one of my past spiritual directors recommended that I keep a dream journal and pen next to my bed. In those groggy moments between sleep and wakefulness, whenever remnants of a dream linger in my mind, I force myself to scribble them down in my dream journal. After the first six months of keeping a dream journal, I noticed a pattern. In the majority of my dreams, I am traveling. The people who show up in my dreams change, but my role in navigating through unknown lands stays the same. It became glaringly clear to me that my soul is on a perpetual search, just like Dorothy in Oz or the Monkey King in *Journey to the West*. What exactly my soul is searching for, I'm not sure, but maybe one day I'll find out.

Paying attention to our dreams reminds us that our souls are quite adept at imagining odd scenarios that can even defy the scientific properties and limitations of our earthly existence. Dreams are also where the Spirit or our ancestors can remind us of who we are and pass on to us their prayers. In the seasons when I am struggling the most, my grandma tends to show up in my dreams. Since dreams are not restricted by reality, they can spark the ability to imagine what may seem impossible.

Sharing Our Collective Imagination

Finally, imagining must be a communal posture. As BIPOC individuals in particular, we may not have our own capacity to see beyond reality, because in a white-dominated society, our communities are constantly being told what and how to see. So we need to imagine together and help one another see where our imaginations are restricted. On the days when I can't imagine for myself, I hope that you can and will imagine for me. And if we want a different kind of community, then we have to develop a shared imagination and carry it forward. De La Torre writes, "The difficult task for the colonized is to learn how to think new thoughts in a way that is less a response and more an indigenous radical worldview different from the normative philosophies that have historically justified our subservient place within society."[6] This shift in expressing a radical

worldview, however, cannot be done alone. To discover a
new way of being in community and to build a new kind
of society, we must imagine as a community. We need to
share our dreams with one another and discover the areas
where our dreams overlap. Through our shared imagination, we also discover each person's unique gifts and con-
tributions and how we may work together.

Imagination is our souls' way of seeing. Our capacity to
imagine is magical because we can see things that don't yet
exist; thus, it is a sacred spiritual posture. Although there
is much work to do to unform the white superiority in our
imaginations, we can engage this unforming collectively by
encouraging one another to imagine. Imagination helps us
shift, then, into an experienced spirituality as our bodies
move into a new way of being.

For Reflection and Discussion

1. How did you play pretend as a child?
2. In what ways have the realities and practicalities
   of the world suppressed your imagination?
3. What are your reoccurring dreams, and what do
   they speak to you?
4. Remember a moment in your childhood when
   you were the most carefree. What were you doing?
   What were you like? Imagine who you would be
   today if you could be more like your childhood self.
5. What do you imagine for your community five
   years from now and ten years from now? What is
   it like? What are you doing together? What is your
   role in the community?

5

LANGUAGE

Developing an active, supernatural connection with the Spirit begins with these questions: Do you believe God speaks? Do you believe we as human beings can encounter and have conversations with the Creator? And does God have something to say in our times? If your answer is yes, then these are the next questions you must ask yourself: How do I listen? How do I meet with God? How we answer these questions determines how we pray.

As social beings, we all learn ways to communicate, and yet I am fascinated by the thousands of languages that have developed through human history, demonstrating our diversity and creativity. These languages are not just verbal but also nonverbal. Language unites us as distinct communities, and at the same time, it can divide us into separate communities. Language mediates our connections to one another, and in the spiritual life, language also mediates our relationship with God. In addition to using verbal language, most human cultures develop different rituals and practices in our attempts to communicate with the divine. We may long to share with God our desires and needs, and we want to hear God's desires for us. I believe no single cultural or religious tradition can teach us how

to communicate with God or how God speaks. God is so
big that we need to hear and learn from one another to
piece together the many ways that God speaks and inter-
acts with humanity. We need to expand our posture of
language to expand how we pray.

In the United States, we teach our children a transmitter cultural orientation.[1] In a transmitter orientation, it
is the speaker's responsibility to communicate their message clearly. If there's miscommunication, it's the speaker's
fault. Other cultures, however, form children in a receiver
cultural orientation. In these cultures, it is the listener's
responsibility to understand the message being communicated. Those of us who have grown up in a receiver-
orientated culture learn to read body language, cultural
expectations, emotional expressions, and what's *not* being
said to receive and interpret the message. Receiver-oriented
cultures socially form children in nonverbal communica-
tion to a much greater degree than transmitter-oriented
cultures. In the Asian American community, this ability is
known as the "Asian sixth sense."

As Christianity developed in a transmitter orientation,
it became a faith bounded by verbal language, particularly
Western languages. In a transmitter faith, those who are
trained to preach and teach have the full authority to
speak about God; thus spiritual formation is often taught
by the educated for the educated, myself included. African theologian Herbert Moyo writes, "The colonial liturgy
located God in books: to understand God, one had to read
the Bible, the hymns, and the leitourgia. To worship God,
one had to first get a Western education. Books deprived
the illiterate of access to God."[2] A transmitter spirituality
gives power to the educated to speak about God and determine how we all connect with God.

My maternal grandmother was illiterate. She was born into a very poor family in Taiwan. At a young age, she was sold to another family to work as a servant in their household. In my twenties, I lived with my grandma in Taiwan for six months. We spent every morning together walking through the daily market and eating breakfast. One time, my grandma came with me to church because I was preaching that day. With her presence there, I suddenly saw our typical Sunday service from a whole new perspective. So much of the service was reliant on reading through the liturgy, worship, and Scripture. Even more, we have our own Christian vocabulary with terms that aren't used in everyday life. Afterward, my grandma commented on my body language and the strength of my voice. What do faith and spiritual formation look like for someone like my grandma, who did not have the privilege of education? When Scripture reading isn't possible and sermons are usually too academic to follow, does that mean my grandma does not have an active faith? Does that mean my grandma can never know God? That experience forever changed the way I preach. Each time I prepare a sermon now, I assume my grandma is listening, because maybe someone like my grandma is listening.

Sojourner Truth (1797–1883) was a different kind of preacher compared to seminary-educated preachers. Born into slavery, Sojourner Truth was also illiterate, and yet she lived the second half of her life as a preacher and activist. She regularly spoke on behalf of the abolitionist movement and the women's suffrage movement. The first time I read about her life, my seminary-educated mind immediately questioned, How could she be a preacher if she never read the Scriptures? What if she preached false theology? The answer, of course, is that she listened to the Scriptures. In fact, her biographer wrote that she had children read to her. Historian Nell Irvin Painter writes, "Truth examined the scriptures by hearing them, and she preferred children rather than adults as readers. Children, she said, would reread the same passage as many times as she requested without adding commentary, but adults began to explain when she asked for repetition."[3] I am very much like the adults Sojourner encountered. I read the Scriptures with my mind, and I'm quick to interpret their meaning. Sojourner Truth practiced a slow hearing of the Scriptures and wasn't afraid to listen over and over again until she could fully receive the words. Even more, Truth believed in the active empowerment of the Holy Spirit within her to help her understand and interpret the words. In fact, she liked to say to her friends, "You read books; God himself talks to me."[4]

Westernized Christians are unable to trust that other peoples have other ways of wisdom that have nothing to do with formal education. There are facets of God we can't understand with our minds or describe with words but must be experienced with our whole being. Liturgy can be read, but liturgy can also be embodied. There are experiences of God that we can't name or give words to, and I don't think we need to. God can be sensed, practiced, felt, experienced. We need a receiver orientation of prayer to fully experience God.

In a Western transmitter orientation, we become the main speakers of prayer and the main definers of God. Verbal practices become our primary ways of communicating with God. I have often heard prayer described as *talking to God*. This notion of prayer often becomes a one-directional conversation in which we do all the talking, which allows us to control prayer and to control

God. What if prayer is not just talking to God? What if prayer is our full-body experience of God? We need to expand our posture of prayer in order to experience God in new ways.

Our Universal Language

We often experience God in silence rather than words. Sometimes the silence of God is painful, especially when we desperately need to know that God is near and active in our world. But after many years of complaining to God about God's silent treatment, I realized that maybe I've misunderstood God all along. Maybe God's preferred language is silence, and I need to learn God's language instead of expecting God to speak my language.

When I stare at the stars on a dark and quiet night, God seems to have plenty to say. Psalm 19 says,

> The heavens declare the glory of God;
>   the skies proclaim the work of his hands.
> Day after day they pour forth speech;
>   night after night they reveal knowledge.
> They have no speech, they use no words;
>   no sound is heard from them.
> Yet their voice goes out into all the earth,
>   their words to the ends of the world.

Our experience of God's silence does not mean God has nothing to say or refuses to speak. God's silence is not a void; it's not an empty silence. Rather, it's a thick silence. It's the same silence in which the stars and skies communicate so loudly and clearly.

Perhaps God's primary language is silence because God much prefers our presence over our words. Because our words are so limited, for us to get a full experience of God, maybe only silence will do. Gustavo Gutiérrez writes, "And when words are incapable of showing forth our experience, we fall back on symbols, which are another way of remaining silent. For when we use a symbol, we do not speak; we let an object or gesture speak for us. This is precisely how we proceed in the liturgy; symbolic language is the language of a love that transcends words."[5] Our spiritual formation should form us not to speak a standard set of belief statements but to listen for God's language. When our words cannot express our prayers, then we lean back into that silence and pray through symbols, metaphors, movements, and presence.

God's sacred silence is not the absence of language but the fullness of presence. It forms us in a posture of listening, seeing, and being with one another before trying to define one another. It is a universal language shared by all people and all creation. To discover where our diverse cultural and spiritual traditions meet, we begin with this common language. From a shared silence, we discover our common prayers; even through language barriers, we share common needs, emotions, and desires.

We live in a society that has a contentious relationship with silence. Our modern society tends to avoid silence in favor of more and more information. Silence can be traumatic, as it often forces us to face ourselves, our pasts, and God. Silence can also be weaponized, as oppressed people have continuously been silenced and not given the opportunity to speak. Therefore, we must first unform the harm caused by silencing and slowly trust that in the silence with God, we are not diminished but fully seen and heard. God does not need verbal language to hear our hearts. Through prayer, we become more and more comfortable with being present to our sacred selves and with God without needing to fill the space with words. Slowly, we learn that God's silence is safe because it offers rest. As a spiritual director, I subtly train my directees to be comfortable with silence because that is often the space where the most transformation occurs. Each time we meet, I may let the silence linger just a few seconds longer. The silence teaches us not to fix our problems but to listen to them. Silence places us in a receiving posture.

Prayer as Rest

In the fourth century, a remarkable contemplative movement formed in the desert region in and around Egypt and Syria. Men and women, now known as the Desert Fathers and Mothers, flocked to the desert in their search for God. These contemplative activists were resisting the increasingly institutionalized and politicized movement of Christianity centered in Rome. So they went to listen for God in the deep silence of the desert. The Desert Mothers and Fathers believed that prayer had nothing to do with talking to God. Instead, they experienced prayer as resting in God.[6]

Perhaps you are in a season of not knowing what to say to God. In prayer, we don't need to say anything at all. Rather, prayer is a body posture and heart posture of finding rest in God's presence. This means that a good night's sleep can be a form of prayer too. We may find that our souls resist and avoid silence because it is a vulnerable space. In prayer, we may simply look at ourselves and allow God to look at us. That can feel vulnerable. As silence places us in such a receiving posture, however, we then give space for God to act, to speak, to surprise us. When we settle into that safe space of just looking at one another, we will find both God and our selves.

Discernment

Because of our Western understanding of prayer as a verbal conversation with God, one of the most common questions I hear about prayer is "How do I know if I'm hearing God's voice and not my own?" But I don't believe that's the most helpful question to ask, because it implies that our own voices are wrong and bad. I don't believe that is true. Western theology has overemphasized original sin and, in so doing, led to teachings that our desires and wants are sinful. We forget, however, that in the creation narrative, before original sin, there was original goodness. We can trust our ability to discern what is right and good. In discernment, then, we are not listening for God's voice over our own. We may not be listening for a voice at all. Rather, we listen for where our own desires and the Spirit's desires align.

Discernment is not a spiritual practice we use only when we have a big decision to make. Rather, discernment is learning to recognize our own voices and the Spirit's voice in the same way we recognize the voices of those we love most. We listen not just through words but also through emotions, actions, and silences. We practice listening for the desires and wants that are stirring in us. We listen for God's heart and desires for us. Because our capacity to discern grows out of our familiarity with God and self, discernment can't happen in a day or when we have a major decision to make but must be cultivated over time. We learn to listen for the Spirit's voice as she whispers within us. The more we listen, the more we will become familiar with her presence and ways of communicating.

In the Western church, teachings on discernment often assume individual agency and power, and thus, discernment is focused on decision-making and actions. This understanding of discernment leaves out those who do not always have the privilege and power of choice. Discernment is not decision-making. Rather, discernment is allowing God to show us who we are to be in this world. Maybe God doesn't care much about what you do but cares a great deal about the kind of person you are. If we know who we are to be, we will also know how we are to act. Sometimes we listen for how we can best respond as compassionate human beings. Sometimes we listen for the path ahead that is the most loving and the least harmful. Discernment is a posture of listening that helps us grow into the person that God knows us to be.

An individualistic understanding of discernment also disregards those who live in communal cultures, in which one's family and community speak into one's life. But discernment is not just individual; it is a collective posture of listening. In a communal practice of discernment, we can take time to listen together and to listen on one another's behalf. We remind one another of who God created us to be. In a communal discernment, we ask who our families and our communities are and should be. In a collective discernment, we also consider our own roles within the family and community and the ways our individual lives impact the greater whole. We also allow the elders in our communities to provide their deep wisdom and to teach us our collective identity.

Prayer as our full-body experiences of God opens us to experience God in new ways as we are present to God, and God is present to us. We can connect with the divine Spirit through the languages of silence, symbols, movements, and emotions. Prayer allows us to settle into God's continual presence and find our rest there.

For Reflection and Discussion

1. Did you grow up in a transmitter-oriented culture or a receiver-oriented culture?
2. What are the ways in which one prays with a transmitter orientation? How does one pray with a receiver orientation?
3. How have you experienced God in silence?
4. Think of a time when God communicated with you. How did you recognize God?
5. How have you experienced discernment in community?

6

WORK/REST

My family has a common Asian immigrant story. In the mid-1970s, my eldest aunt and uncle immigrated from Taiwan to the American suburbs, and they opened a Chinese restaurant. They also made the way for their parents and younger siblings, including my parents, to immigrate. My parents worked as waiters at the restaurant before they moved on to their own careers. All my life, I've watched my aunts and uncles fall asleep on the couch during our family gatherings, usually after dinner. Having extra days off during the American holidays forces them to stop after working long hours and full weeks. As soon as they stop, though, their aching, overworked bodies realize how they long for sleep.

As I reflect on my family's story, I often wonder, What spiritual practices of rest and work are meaningful for immigrant families? Most spiritual formation resources address the important spiritual practices of rest and keeping Sabbath. We may take time away and also engage in practices of self-care, and of course, that is necessary and healthy. But a Western approach to rest comes out of an individualistic perspective of spiritual formation. We live in a world where not everyone has the privilege and

opportunity to rest or get away, however. Gustavo Gutiérrez writes that our literature on spirituality is largely created
for the privileged who do not have to worry about food
and housing.[1] Our current spiritual formation resources
alienate the working class. I think of the many immigrant
parents I know who work long hours and cannot get away
to recuperate. I think of those who work multiple part-
time jobs without getting paid time off. What does spiritual
formation mean for those who are exhausted and overworked but don't have the privilege of self-care? We need
in our formation liberative spiritual practices of work and
rest that are not just for the privileged but for the poor, for
the immigrants, for the working class.

Work and rest are justice issues that affect our everyday
spiritual formation. We all work in a corrupt economic
system that runs on constant greed and production, but
the working poor and immigrant families particularly
bear the burdens of this corrupt system. We cannot rest
well unless we unform our distorted practices of work.
We also cannot truly find rest as individuals until all in
the community can also find rest. In the Old Testament
Scriptures, the commandment to keep the Sabbath was
not just an order to rest. Rather, the Sabbath establishes
a liberative spiritual practice to address our unjust and
unethical systems of work.

Sabbath as a Collective Posture

Biblical scholar Walter Brueggemann compares our
unhealthy relationships to work with the system of slavery
in Egypt.[2] In such a system, people are not viewed as people; they become machines to increase the wealth of those

in power. In such a system, there is no rest. In Egypt, the Israelites do not keep Sabbath. Slaves do not rest, and even the land doesn't rest.[3] There is around-the-clock activity and production. Brueggemann writes that an economy that does not recognize Sabbath leads to forms of violence and abuse because workers are treated as commodities rather than human beings who need rest.[4] Our economic system today is no different from the violence of slavery in Egypt. We require the nonstop labor of immigrants and the working poor to continuously feed a system based on greed. This system is violent, as those with wealth and power control our work and rest. We need the working class, and yet we don't protect the workers. We dehumanize people as machines.

The Sabbath laws establish a new rhythm of life for the Israelites after they are freed from Egypt. The Sabbath laws counteract the unjust and abusive economic system of slavery. The way of Sabbath is detailed in the fourth commandment in Deuteronomy 5:12–15:

> Observe the Sabbath day by keeping it holy, as the Lord your God has commanded you. Six days you shall labor and do all your work, but the seventh day is a sabbath to the Lord your God. On it you shall not do any work, neither you, nor your son or daughter, nor your male or female servant, nor your ox, your donkey or any of your animals, nor any foreigner residing in your towns, so that your male and female servants may rest, as you do. Remember that you were slaves in Egypt and that the Lord your God brought you out of there with a mighty hand and an outstretched arm. Therefore the Lord your God has commanded you to observe the Sabbath day.

In this passage, Moses explains to the Israelites that they can rest now because they've been saved from the economic oppression of slavery.[5] They no longer have to live according to that violent rhythm of production. Sabbath breaks the nonstop, violent cycle of production and consumption. It breaks our greed by forcing us to stop continually trying to do more and gain more. The Sabbath system is a just and equal system because all—animals, land, landowners, servants, and foreigners—enjoy the same rest. None of us has ever truly experienced a Sabbath, however, because we still live in a world where foreigners, servants, land, and animals do not get sufficient rest. Imagine a world where we all had equal rest.

The Old Testament laws inaugurate not just a Sabbath day but a Sabbath year once every seven years (Exod 23:10–11; Deut 15:1). In a Sabbath year, debts are canceled, and all agricultural work stops. This Sabbath involves our relationships to one another and our relationships to the earth. In a Sabbath year, we engage in an economic spiritual practice by canceling debts. The land also rests from our constant production. A Sabbath year requires that we trust the grace of the earth to provide enough for a year, no more or less. If our land is supposed to rest every seventh year, the fact that we have worked our lands for centuries without Sabbath means they are grossly exploited.

Beyond the Sabbath year, a full social and economic Sabbath—a jubilee, a year of liberation—is announced every fifty years (Lev 25:10). I like to think of jubilee as a big red reset button. In this Sabbath, all hired workers and servants are released.[6] Everyone can also buy back ancestral lands they may have lost. This Sabbath gives those who have lost everything a chance to restart, and it requires the privileged—those who have gained more land, wealth, or workers—to let go. Jubilee is the ultimate expression of the radical liberation of Sabbath. The Sabbath cycles of days, years, and jubilee form a communal rhythm that ensures economic justice.

The Western church has taught Sabbath keeping as an individual practice of taking a day off and missed the understanding of Sabbath as a collective posture that orients us toward a just society where all can find rest. Therefore, even as our individual rest is important, we also need to help others in our communities to rest. Keeping the Sabbath rhythm requires everyone in the community, including those with privilege and power, to participate so that all can rest. The practice of communal rest is meant to train us into a way of living as a society. As someone who is privileged to take days off and go on retreats, I need to look at my community. These are questions I've found helpful to ask myself: Who can I free to rest? Who is exhausted? Who is not getting enough rest? And what little part can I do to help lessen their load so they can rest too?

Letting Go

The Sabbath system requires a regular rhythm of letting go. A corrupt economy is about production and gain; rest is letting go. Canceling debts, releasing servants, and allowing the land to rest are radical spiritual practices to resist hoarding and building up wealth. In the Scriptures, work and rest are not opposites. Together, they create a cyclical rhythm, a continual embodied movement of unforming and re-forming. As we enter into rest, we unform through practices of letting go. We then experience a holy rest through the practice of stopping. When it is time to work again, we carry our holy rest into our work. Rest is the center of this rhythm, and work flows in and out of our rest.

But we tend to get one part wrong. We have made work, rather than rest, the center of our weekly rhythms, so we rest from our work. And from that one change, the whole rhythm becomes distorted. Our identities become tied to our work, our family lives revolve around work schedules, and those imbalances ripple out into our unjust economy, which abuses work. When work is the center, then even if we take a day off, we are restless, because our minds, spirits, and bodies are still lingering in our work instead of being present to our rest. We are still thinking about what didn't get done and what we have to do when we get back to work.[7] Often, we are forced to rest from sheer exhaustion and burnout. But resting from exhaustion is not a sustainable rhythm, because we never practice letting go. And we may never receive a holy rest.

If work is the center of our rhythms, our souls may try to get something out of our work that indifferent systems of work cannot give to us. When I sit with my directees, I notice that work is one of the most common topics of conversation. We may seek from our work a sense of purpose and worth. And every time we don't get that from our jobs, we feel distress not just in our bodies but also in our souls. So we try to use our work to advance ourselves, to promote ourselves, to distinguish ourselves. And suddenly, we find ourselves trapped in an economic system of competition and greed that never stops. For others of us, our sense of obligation, responsibility, and pride in our work means that we have trouble letting go of work and creating rhythms of rest. We may get caught up in anxiety, performance, and perfection. We sacrifice our health and well-being for the sake of a never-ending commitment to work.

BIPOC communities may experience an additional weariness as we navigate our work in white institutions. To constantly code switch from our cultural ways of being to the expectations of white organizations takes extra energy. We may also be called upon to do additional, often unpaid, work to help our companies or institutions address issues of race. When my BIPOC directees talk about their work lives, I find we cannot disconnect their experiences from the systemic and cultural oppression ingrained in their workplaces. Our workplaces may be hostile environments for BIPOC employees whose experiences of racism may get dismissed. We get worn down over years of having to work harder in a system where BIPOC individuals get paid less and are overlooked for leadership.

Even the church reinforces an unhealthy relationship with work. I used to work with a church plant where our team measured our success by attendance. My own identity and self-worth became tied to the number of people who showed up at prayer or Bible study each week. I interpreted the lack of attendance as people not taking their faith and God seriously. When I started working outside of the church and went home after a long day of work, however, I suddenly understood why it was so hard to motivate people to show up to church multiple days a week. The issue is not that people aren't taking their faith seriously; they're just exhausted. An event-based church, dependent on attending programs and volunteering, becomes just another job to juggle with our work lives and family responsibilities. The rhythms of the church don't match the rhythms of people's lives. Churches aren't known as places of rest; instead, we are just as busy in the church as we are at work. People burning out from never-ending church events indicates there is something seriously wrong with our understanding of Sabbath.

We need to continually unform the effects of our distorted economic system that have become ingrained in our thinking, habits, and rhythms. We need a rhythm that centers around rest—a radical practice that counteracts the unhealthy rhythms of our work by freeing us from performance, constant production, and proving ourselves to others. Without this daily and weekly rhythm of letting go, our rest is limited and temporary. Through rest, we unform the economic values of competition, scarcity, abuse, and greed.

In letting go, we acknowledge what we can't do—and what we need God to do. Rabbi Abraham Heschel writes, "Rest on the Sabbath as if all your work were done."[8] Rest is knowing we've done what we could do this week, and now we need to receive grace. Rest is the center and heart of our work because it acknowledges that in the end, no matter how hard we work, we continue to be dependent on the grace of God. Rest unforms the economic abuse in our bodies, and it is also a posture of the soul and mind. In addition to physical rest, we need internal rest from striving and anxiety—not just a temporary numbing over but an intentional time to reconnect with God and self.

Holy Rest

A true Sabbath rest, a holy rest, is present when we stop after letting go. We stop to look at God, just as God stopped to look at us on the seventh day of creation. I believe God continues to keep Sabbath even to this day. In our mutual gaze with God, we find a holy rest because God does not see us as utilities or machines for production. To stop is to resist the way the world uses our bodies for labor. To stop is to acknowledge that people are more important than production. Stopping can be so unfamiliar to our bodies, however, that some of us need to practice stopping daily. Howard Thurman writes, "Sometime during each day, everything should stop and the art of being still must be practiced. For some temperaments, it will not be easy because the entire nervous system and body have been geared over the years to activity, to overt and tense functions."[9] Some of us have not truly rested in a very, very long time, because our bodies and minds do not actually stop.

In the spiritual life, we need to be formed to find our rest here, exactly where we live every day, and not just when we have the time or privilege to get away. We need to recognize that those who cannot attend Sunday services or who are too exhausted to engage in Bible studies and spiritual practices may have other ways of connecting to the sacred. Rest can be found through simple practices. For those who most need sleep on their Sabbath, sleeping is a holy physical practice, as it unforms the exhaustion of our work and restores our bodies. The practice of stopping also allows us to be fully present with our families and loved ones. We experience a holy rest when we realize we don't have to do or accomplish anything at all. Our identities and worth are found in God's loving gaze.

For immigrant families, rest may be limited. My prayer for immigrant parents is that they can find rest in the truth that their worth is not defined by the success or failure of their work. I also pray that they find a space where they can take a break from navigating unfamiliar white systems. BIPOC and immigrant communities experience rest through places and spaces where white Western norms are not the center and places where our own stories and cultural expressions are centered. Especially when we live in a world that daily denies our dignity and sacredness, we find rest with the families and communities that reflect our sacredness back to us.

Good Work

Rest is a way of being that we can carry even into our work, as it helps us let go of any unhealthy attachments we may have to work. Who we are in our rest determines who we are in the world. If we know our Sabbath identities, we avoid dehumanizing other people for their labor and production. We respect and encourage rest in others. When rest is the center, we continuously draw from that infinite resource of rest in God. As we take time in our rest to unform our distorted relationships with work, we then experience an integrated rhythm of good work and rest.

I think we can tell whether pastors and other leaders find their identities in their ministries or in their Sabbaths, whether their identities come from their roles, authority, titles, and accomplishments or from their intimate connections with God. These are the questions we need to ask ourselves: What's happening in my Sabbath? What is the identity that I carry into my work? And how do I continually draw from my Sabbath identity as I work?

Western spirituality does not always acknowledge the formation that may happen in and through our work, where we spend most of our time. Work is part of our experienced spirituality in which we connect to the sacred through our labors and creativity. Through good work and good rest, we honor our human abilities and skills. Approaching work as a spiritual posture enables us to be attentive to the good work we are doing. One helpful practice is to slow down our work and focus on one task at a time. Through this practice, we can be wholeheartedly present to each task as a form of prayer through our bodies.

Working to survive and to provide for our families are also honorable practices, but this message is missing from our church pulpits. The church tends to look at work from the perspective of the privileged. A word such as *calling* implies that we have a choice in how we spend our time, but it alienates those without that privilege, those who simply work to pay the bills and to put food on the table. We need to recognize that this, too, is good work.

In my childhood memories, my dad smelled like motor oil. He worked as a mechanical engineer in a manufacturing plant and spent his days fixing machines. Even in his free time, my dad was usually in the garage, bent over the engine of a car or rolled underneath one. Church services were not created for people like my dad. He felt inferior in a church filled with doctors and professors. He didn't feel comfortable praying or attending Bible studies among those with higher education. It was not until late in life that my dad found his place in the church. He started fixing cars and unclogging sinks for members of the immigrant church. He finally felt like his work contributed something to his community and for the first time experienced belonging. For a short while, he served as deacon of member care because the pastor realized he visited more families than any other deacon or elder. My dad left the deacon role after one term because he couldn't tolerate sitting through the long meetings with other deacons and elders. He figured he could still engage in "member care" without being required to attend monthly meetings. Although my dad felt belittled in the church because he worked with machines, he experienced his creativity and good work whenever he found new ways of fixing things.

In the cycle of rest/work, the stillness of rest can stir a greater creativity in our work. Work not only refers to the tasks that pay the bills but is also found in what inspires our creativity. Our work is to be cocreators in whatever opportunities are given to us—in the kitchen, in our conversations, in the garage, in our writing, in all sorts of human endeavors that our modern economy may not recognize as work. When work is a spiritual posture, we all participate in the ongoing, communal work of creating. We all need to find ways to settle into our physical, mental, and spiritual rest in our everyday lives in order to allow the creative movements of the Spirit to stir in us. Rest is a receiving posture that then allows us to move into the everyday creativity of our work.

For Reflection and Discussion

1. Is work or rest at the center of your weekly rhythms? How do you work in and out of your rest?
2. How are you being oppressed by systems of work?
3. When do you feel the most rested?
4. Who are you in your Sabbath?
5. In what ways do you express your creativity in your work?

PART 3

Orientation ⇌ Collective

We all long for intimate relationships in which we are truly seen, heard, and known. In the West, however, we have developed an event-based way of being in community.[1] Church has become synonymous with attending worship services, Bible studies, or special classes or volunteering. We have also turned the commandment to "love your neighbor" into service projects and outreach events. When the event is over, we all return to our own homes and lock the door. This event-based way of forming community can feel insufficient for our needs for deep relationships. I believe that the church today has largely failed to create or be the kind of community that we all long for.

The history of Western church architecture reflects this shift into an event-based faith as we went from meeting in homes, where we shared a meal, to basilicas and cathedrals, where we sit in rows and face an altar. We became spectators of our faith. The Protestant Reformation brought an additional focus on word and preaching. Over time, Sunday services became centered around preaching, particularly by ordained or educated clergy. This focus on preaching by an individual further distanced us from a communal experience.

In the history of Evangelicalism, the revivals that started in the mid-eighteenth century further reinforced the role of preacher as performer, and by the nineteenth century, we adapted theater spaces and auditoriums for use as sanctuaries.[2] Pulpits and stages center our eyes and ears on a sole actor, and the weekly sermon and worship become a show. The pastor's self-identity can become tied to their preaching and production, and they are often evaluated and criticized by the congregation based on their performance.

An event-based community is unhealthy for the congregation as well as the pastor. We often feel guilty when we're too tired or busy to be as involved as we're expected to be when being "a good Christian" seems to depend on attendance. Members can falsely think that simply attending events is enough for our own growth and formation. We place the responsibility for our souls' health on the pastor (a.k.a. "the event planner") and not ourselves. We can become passive observers of our faith. We need to let go of these Western-built structures and measurements of what it means to be the church. Perhaps community was never meant to be built on attending events. Western attempts to create community are constantly thwarted because an event-based community expects to grow bigger and to create better productions. An event-based community centers around individual leaders rather than the whole. Whenever a problem arises, we may address them by creating another event or a new program.

Despite all this effort to create a Sunday service "experience," many congregations have failed to facilitate genuine community. Relationships in event-based communities feel transactional. Members are valued for attendance and serving at events, but these events do not necessarily facilitate connection. Sadly, one can walk in and out of a church service and never be acknowledged. An event-based way of church has been carried over into non-Western churches, creating an awkward expression of community in traditionally communal cultures where community happens naturally on the streets, in plazas and parks, and in homes rather than at structured times. The health of our collective soul is withering. The churchless masses long for deep community and experiences of the sacred, but they are not finding it in the institutional church.

The last section of this book is about our collective soul. We are collectively disillusioned. We are collectively lonely. We will continue to feel a void until we attend to our collective well-being. But while we might be aware that something doesn't feel right in our current expressions of community, none of us can create community alone. The only way forward is to imagine and create something new together.

The Inverted Hospitality of Colonization

In collectivist cultures, community is traditionally facilitated through a culture of reciprocal hospitality. Theologian Willie Jennings observes, however, that historically, the Western church has practiced an "inverted hospitality."[3] He writes, "It claimed to be the host, the owner of the spaces it entered, and demanded native peoples enter its cultural logics, its ways of being in the world, and its conceptualities." An inverted hospitality is one-directional. The host controls how the hospitality is offered and how it is to be received. The host maintains power in the relationship. In the church today, we continue this inverted hospitality whenever we use hospitality as a tool for evangelism, outreach, or church growth, expecting others to conform to our own expectations.

Many of us practice a one-directional hospitality. We may like being affirmed for our generosity and recognized for our service. When it comes time to be the recipient of hospitality, however, we resist. We take pride in our self-reliance, and receiving hospitality makes us feel vulnerable. The need for perfection further distorts an inverted hospitality. When we become obsessed with presenting a tidy home and preparing good food, we might no longer be offering hospitality. When caught up in perfection, our souls are no longer present to the community but focused on ourselves and our own performances. We might hide behind our busywork. An event-based community reduces hospitality to entertaining and throwing dinner parties. The hosts may feel overwhelmed just thinking about how to create the perfect event. Hospitality, however, is not about serving food and cleaning up.

Patriarchal cultures may also misinterpret hospitality as "sacrificial service." The male leaders who endorse this faulty definition, however, all too conveniently leave the work of "hospitality" to the women. In the Asian immigrant church, this means the women of the church are busy preparing and serving lunch every Sunday and cleaning up after the congregation. Sundays are not restful for the women of the church.

Individualist cultures, therefore, should not be teaching the global church about community or hospitality. We need to unform this historical misuse of hospitality in the church. Hospitality is not an event or a practice; it is a cultural way of being in community that we need to learn from collectivist cultures.

Cultivating Hospitality

Hospitality is a posture of openness with which the hosts share of themselves to create an environment where others feel comfortable sharing of themselves too. It is facilitated through the sharing of food, space, and embodied practices that invite the opening of our souls to another. We can all think of people in our lives who exemplify hospitality for us. These friends or family are more than the foods they make or the gifts they give; rather, they have a heart of hospitality. They have a way of inviting us to be ourselves and to feel like we're home. They offer an openness in times of need even if they are unprepared. They welcome us into the messiness of their lives and share whatever they may have to give. Those who have cultivated a hospitable spirit tend to draw people to them.

Ironically, hospitality is a space we need to create within ourselves before we can offer that space to others. Cultivating hospitality begins in our own souls and flows outward. In that space between us and God, we experience the deepest hospitality. We are invited into the intimate community of the divine Trinity. There we can be open, honest, vulnerable. We are invited to find our rest there whenever we are weary. As we enter God's Trinitarian hospitality, we are able to be hospitable to ourselves. If we respond to ourselves like an unwelcoming host, with criticism and blame, then we will have difficulty extending genuine hospitality to others. But when we find our acceptance and belonging in our own souls between ourselves and God, then an amazing thing happens. We find that our souls expand, and we have room in our souls to let others in.

We all need to cultivate this hospitable posture of the soul in order to facilitate healthy community with one another. If we do not, if we need to look outside of our souls for acceptance and security, then we will be unable to offer others a genuine hospitability. We will be afraid of being too open for fear of being rejected. We will have little capacity to let others in, because we'll be so preoccupied with how we present ourselves and what others think of us. We will be so self-focused in our interactions with others that we will be perpetually thinking about our own stories, opinions, and responses rather than truly receiving and listening to another person. If our souls are unhealthy, we will ooze that unhealthiness into our community. Cultivating an inner hospitality frees us to offer an open, nonjudgmental space for others.

For some people, the thought of community, especially religious community, brings up memories of hurtful experiences, even trauma. Perhaps this has been your story. Your heart is cynical, and you feel guarded against opening up to community again. Your spiritual practice in this season is to fully acknowledge the pain you've experienced because of others. Recognize the holy wisdom in you that told you something was wrong. Honor your decision to speak up or to stay silent. Acknowledge the courage it took for you to leave an unhealthy or abusive community. Grieve the loss of friends who once supported you. You need to recognize those seasons when you may not have space for others. In those seasons, draw back to where it's just you and God again and take the time you need to cultivate hospitality by receiving hospitality. Take as long as you need to heal your soul. When you begin to sense your need and longing for community once again, then you can venture out slowly and carefully.

Each time we allow someone new into our soul space, we are taking a risk, but sharing our souls with another is the first step toward forming community. Hospitality facilitates seeing and being seen, listening and being listened to, knowing and being known, caring and being cared for. So to receive hospitality, we need to ask ourselves, Are we willing to be seen, to be listened to, to be known, and to be cared for? How might we risk sharing more of ourselves in order to allow others to truly know us? At the same time, to facilitate reciprocal hospitality, we discern how we may see, listen to, know, and care for others. How might we create an open space within ourselves to be an inviting and restful presence for others?

A reciprocal hospitality is able to both offer and receive. This means some of us need to practice receiving hospitality and allowing others to take care of us. As we practice receiving, we may feel resistance in our souls; our self-sufficient natures may want to take over and refuse help. This resistance is our pride. A humble posture recognizes that we all need help, and we all need to be invited into spaces of rest. A reciprocal hospitality is a communal posture. It is facilitated through practices of generosity and kindness but also through the sharing of our needs. As we share our needs with others and allow others to help us, we encourage the ongoing cultivation of hospitality in one another. When we are able to receive hospitality, then the cycle of hospitality is nurtured. Kindness and generosity continue to multiply and expand throughout the community.

Western spirituality has focused on the individual soul, but in a collective cultural orientation, we recognize that we also share a communal body and a collective spirit. Thus, we need communal spiritual postures that attend to our collective health. We need spiritual practices that nurture how we live in community and in relation to one another. Hospitality is the start of a collective spirituality because it opens us to others and teaches us how to be present to one another. The following postures of dependence, elders, and harmony continue to nurture our collective soul.

For Reflection and Discussion

1. What have been your experiences in event-based churches?
2. How does your culture or family practice hospitality?
3. Where have you experienced hospitality recently? How were you invited into that space?
4. Do you have space in your soul for others in this season? How can you cultivate hospitality in your life?

DEPENDENCE

Cultural psychologist Richard Nisbett conducted a study to compare early primary readers from the 1930s in the United States to mainland China.[1] In the United States, children read the Dick and Jane series. These are typical sentences:

> See Dick. See Dick run.
> See Jane. See Jane run. Run, Jane, run![2]

In mainland China, their primary texts include sentences like these:

> Big brother takes care of little brother.
> Big brother loves little brother.[3]

The West taught children verbs and individual agency, while the East taught familial relationships and an obligation to those relationships. Individualistic cultures certainly have many strengths. Children are formed to be independent, to embrace their gifts, and to speak their minds. Children are encouraged to create and find their own identities. As we grow older, we learn that decisions are our own

to make, and each person has agency and power to make
those decisions. In my American education, I constantly
felt the encouragement to develop my gifts and to stand
out. Even now in the working world, I see that success is
often measured by one's ability to promote oneself and distinguish oneself.

Individualism naturally creates an independent faith.
We think religious beliefs are determined by one's individual and private decision. Spiritual formation becomes
one's personal process of growth and rest. This individuality is reflected in our contemporary spirituality, in which
we are all learning to take care of ourselves, especially our
bodies. This is a good thing. This emphasis on self-care is
overturning many centuries of a faith disconnected from
our bodies and the abuse we put our bodies through in our
distorted relationships with our work.

A perpetually self-focused spirituality, however, is not
complete, because it ignores our collective soul. Our independent natures may hinder us from acknowledging our
need for others and keep us from practicing the vulner-
ability that is absolutely necessary for forming community. An independent faith has made self-sufficient but
often lonely people. Gustavo Gutiérrez writes in *We
Drink from Our Own Wells* that the privatization of spirituality is dangerous because it can distort what we think
it means to be a follower of Christ. He notes that a privatized or individual spirituality can be shallow because
it turns community into a formality and the postures of
compassion and justice into acts of charity.[4] In individualistic cultures, the self is the center, and even practices
of community are determined by one's own needs. Community is optional and based on convenience. Gutiérrez,
often known as the father of liberation theology, states

that a privatized spirituality is unprepared to address the needs of this world. It does not address the injustices in our communities. A spirituality focused on individual practices and self-care will always be temporary unless we take care of the collective. We need a collective spirituality to engage in movements of liberation.

Collectivist cultures use stories, rituals, and social expectations to form children with a communal identity from the time they are born. Language and stories are used to form us in our interconnectedness. Instead of calling adults "Mister" and "Miss," children learn that everyone is an aunt or uncle, brother or sister, godfather or godmother. We learn to see the world as a large web of interconnected relationships. Michael Battle explains of many African cultures, "African epistemology begins with community and moves to individuality, whereas Western epistemology moves from individuality to community."[5] In other words, children are taught in collective cultures to take their place in the community, and individuality is discovered through one's role in the community. Each person holds a responsibility to the collective. The collective needs to be healthy for each individual within to be healthy.

When I think about collectivist communities, I immediately imagine a ball of tangled yarn. In a collective community, everyone's lives are entangled in everyone else's. This sort of community is messy and complicated. Unhealthy codependent relationships certainly can form in such a community. At the same time, hidden within this complexity is a way of life that teaches us how to be together. Although other writers may use the word *interdependence* to describe this way of community, I use the word *dependence*, because dependence is the spiritual posture we have the most trouble with. Through a posture of dependence, we learn to take our places in an interdependent community.

Just as placing a high value on individuality leads to an independent spirituality, placing a high value on the collective leads to a dependent spirituality. I have found that in the West, we are highly resistant to the idea of dependence. It rubs us the wrong way. It goes against the way society has taught us to be. It goes against the admonitions to "do it yourself" and "just try harder." We don't want to bother or inconvenience others. We assume others will take advantage of us, or we'll appear weak.

I want to reclaim the word *dependence*, because dependence facilitates communities of grace. Dependence is the recognition that we are utterly reliant on the grace and mercy of the earth, and in the same way, we are reliant on the grace of God. Dependence is where the spiritual life begins; we realize that we can't rely on our own efforts, but we need God, creation, and community. We cannot form a sustainable spirituality through our own strong wills. We need a power outside of our own. The only way to experience a deep spirituality is to acknowledge our absolute dependence. Gustavo Gutiérrez taught us that dependence is best cultivated through gratitude.[6] He writes that the most frequent prayers of the poor are prayers of gratitude. Through these prayers, we recognize that "contemplation disposes us to recognize that everything is grace."[7] Through the practice of gratitude, we learn to both lean on grace and extend grace to others.

Just as much as we need divine grace, we also need to live in communities of grace, and the only way to experience deep community is to depend on one another. People in communities of dependence are more likely to see their neighbors' struggles as their own. When tragedy occurs, communities of dependence seem to have more communal practices for helping, mourning, lamenting, and resisting together. Communities of privilege are just as dependent on God and others as underresourced communities. The difference is that the latter communities recognize their dependence, and the former often do not.

Dependence offers great freedom. We are released from the burden of doing everything on our own. A posture of dependence releases us from the constant striving in our culture to achieve because our achievements are accomplished together. A spirituality of dependence acknowledges that despite our best efforts, we all still need others to thrive. Dependence is a spiritual posture of acknowledging those times when we think "I can't" and "I need help." It is not shameful; it is acknowledging that we are human and that we can rely and lean on one another.

I will be the first to confess my own strong will to do everything on my own and to keep my struggles hidden, but I also recognize that such a life is not enough to sustain my soul. I need to put myself in a new posture that opens me further to God and others. I am slowly learning that utter dependence on God is not a weakness. Needing help from others is not a weakness but a gift. If you struggle with dependence, then a valuable spiritual practice for you is to regularly ask for help and allow others to help you. A practice of learning to receive slowly unforms our deeply ingrained self-sufficiency.

Parts of a Whole

Learning to be dependent then helps us take our place in an interdependent community. Recognizing our needs for one another helps us take responsibility for our collective identity and well-being. In an independent spirituality, we approach our decisions from the perspective of self and ask, What do I need? In an interdependent spirituality, we ask, What do *we* need? Desmond Tutu explains how this interdependence is cultivated in African cultures: "In Africa recognition of interdependence is called *ubuntu* in Nguni languages, or *botho* in Sotho, which is difficult to translate into English. It is the essence of being human. It speaks of the fact that my humanity is caught up and inextricably bound up in yours. I am human because I belong."[8] Our human formation always takes place within the complexities of community. I cannot experience rest, healing, or wholeness unless I am also helping those around me to rest, heal, and become whole. I will not have peace until my community is at peace. Part of our collective formation is to see our individual identities within our communal identities and to constantly discern and ask ourselves, Who do we need to be together?

In our modern society, we often live fragmented lives in fragmented communities and try to function with a fragmented soul. As Greek philosophy valued classifying and categorizing, we attempted to separate every species of creation into separate categories. We then expanded our vocabulary to dissect and divide all of life into separate entities. In so doing, we dissected our spirituality by dividing mind and body, emotion and reason, sacred and secular, private and public, spiritual and material, self and community. Through this dichotomizing, our lives became compartmentalized. We live frantic lives jumping from one part of life to another, from one identity to the next, dividing our selves and our time. We live in constant activity, unaware that we were never meant to live as divided, independent selves. Daoist philosopher Chuang Tzu believed that the act of classifying is harmful because it fractures the greater whole and disregards how all things are connected to one another, not separated into categories.[9]

Rather than dividing and classifying the experiences of life into different categories, Daoist philosophers organize the world as parts to a whole. How would our spiritual lives change if we saw all of life as parts of one whole? The movement of the collective spiritual life is to bring our fragmented pieces back together again. In an interdependent community, we all take our place as part of the whole. We are each part of our families, communities, society, nation, and earth. We cannot disconnect from the whole, as we depend on our communities and they depend on us.

Taking Care of Our Collective

Those who grow up in a collectivist culture generally consider how our individual decisions affect the greater whole. My friends in Asia inherently understand that a decision of faith is not private; it is a decision that affects their whole family. Immigrant families practice interdependence when they send financial support back to extended family. Their success, even if minor, is shared with the community. Those of us formed by Western cultural values are accustomed to making self-centric decisions, so we need to be intentional about considering how our actions, decisions, and ways of being affect the greater whole. Being formed in a collectivist culture does present challenges, however. Our interdependence can often feel like an obligation. Social obligations can be abused, and social expectations can become burdens. For this reason, we also need to approach our interdependence as an intentional spiritual posture. We need to notice each time we feel resentful or burdened—and each time we feel cared for and loved. We need to recognize both our limitations and when we're able to give.

In an interdependent spirituality, we can share one another's emotions as a collective prayer. Whenever I notice a strong emotional reaction in myself, I stop to ask, Is it my own, someone else's, or is it collective? If it's my own emotion, then I attend to my needs. If it's someone else's, then I ask, Whose? Then I might reach out to check in. If it's a collective emotion, then I ask, What's happening in our community or society right now? Those collective emotions of grief and anger or joy and gratitude are our shared prayers. By intentionally stopping to feel and embrace the emotion, we can connect to our collective spirit. When we carry these emotions together, we are expressing that the injustices experienced in other parts of our community or nation are not other people's problems but actually *our* problems. Racial issues are not isolated incidents but our collective and shared responsibility. Whenever we feel overwhelmed by the violence and injustices of our world, a communal contemplative practice we can engage in together is to take a moment to enter our space of prayer, take a few deep breaths, then intentionally feel our collective emotions. We might ask ourselves, What does that emotion tell us about our whole, and how do we take care of our collective?

For Reflection and Discussion

1. Did you grow up in an individualist or collectivist culture? Or both? How did an individual or communal culture influence your upbringing?
2. In what ways are you cultivating an independent spirituality? In what ways are you cultivating a dependent spirituality?
3. Share about a time when you needed to be dependent on others. What did you learn about yourself or others during that time?
4. Take a moment to connect to our collective spirit. What collective emotion do you sense right now? What does that emotion tell you about our wholeness as a community? What do *we* need?

（

8

ELDERS

I grew up with my paternal grandmother. I called her
Ahma in Taiwanese. While both of my immigrant parents
were out working long hours, Ahma was my childhood
companion after school and on long summer days. I loved
to follow her around as she constantly kept herself busy
folding laundry or prepping for dinner. She had a constant rhythm of movement around the house. My favor-
ite moments were when she made large batches of mochi
as gifts for family and friends. Every once in a while, she
would hand me the ugly mochi to eat. As she worked,
she also told me stories. Ahma's stories had no action
or drama. Instead, all of her stories were about kindness
and communal dependence. She told me about the many
distant relatives and family friends who helped our family
along the way. She told me about my great-great-uncle who
paid for her education and the church auntie who cared
for the newly arriving immigrants from Taiwan. She made
sure to remind me at the end of every story that our family
wouldn't be here if it weren't for the generosity and kindness of others.

Although these weren't the most exciting stories, they
were formative. Her stories instilled in me that I am part

of a larger web of relationships. The grace and mercy of God often come to us through the kindness of others, and we give the same kindness and generosity whenever we're able. This was the collective spirituality I received from Ahma. The evangelical church taught me that my story as a Christian began with my own private decision to follow Jesus or join the church, but I learned from Ahma that my faith actually began generations earlier and comes from my community.

When I ask Christians of color about their faith, they often begin their story with the spirituality of their grandmas and mothers. It was often the matriarchs who embodied faithful and persistent prayer. Kat Armas writes about the faith of our grandmothers in her book *Abuelita Theology*. She explains, "Abuelita theology stems from the reality that in Latine religious culture, matriarchal figures such as abuelitas preserve and pass along religious traditions, beliefs, practices, and spirituality. They function as 'live-in ministers,' particularly because the privilege to receive 'formal' religious instruction is often unavailable. Thus, abuelitas are the functional priestesses and theologians in our familias."[1] We need to learn from our *abuelitas* and ahmas as they pass down their embodied spiritualities to us. Whether matriarchs or patriarchs, our elders are often the ones who bring the family together, including all the new family who stop by for dinner along the way. They are the storytellers who pass the family's experience of God from one generation to the next.

Thus, we need the important practice of generational storytelling as part of our spiritual formation. Tejana poet Carolina Hinojosa-Cisneros writes that for BIPOC communities, "generational storytelling is survival. It is a preservation of history and a dire act as we witness erasure in textbooks and watch our history recounted by those who tell our stories but have never lived in our skin or embodied the blood of our stories."[2] For BIPOC communities, storytelling can be a spiritual practice of resistance to pass on our experiences and knowings of God that may not be taught in the Western church. Storytelling allows children in all cultures to grow up knowing their elders and ancestors. In the West, the art and practice of storytelling have not been incorporated into our spirituality, our church services, liturgies, prayers, or small groups. Thus, we may be missing out on a practice that allows our familial stories to form our souls.

In the West, we often see our immediate family as independent family units, but in collective cultures, the concept of family includes elders, extended family, and close family friends as well as neighbors. Ada María Isasi-Díaz writes, "To understand better the kind of *familia* that is Hispanic women's realm, we need to see how in Latina culture the community is an extension, a continuation of the family."[3] Each immediate family is just one part of the whole family. Community and family are actually the same. In this larger understanding of "family," there is a communal parenting model, as children are raised by the community and not just their parents. It becomes the responsibility of community elders to pass onto children their belonging and identity within the community.

Spiritual Elders

Early in Jesus's formation, we meet his spiritual grandpa and grandma in Luke chapter 2. Mary and Joseph bring the baby Jesus to the temple for the ritual act of presenting the firstborn to the Lord. As soon as they enter the temple, they are welcomed by Simeon and Anna. Simeon waited his whole life for this moment, and when we meet him in the story, he is nearing death. In a rare occurrence before Acts, the Holy Spirit shows up in this story and stirs Simeon to meet the baby Jesus. As an elder, Simeon offers a prophecy over the baby and to his mother, Mary. Then a rare female prophetess, Anna, who was eighty-four, approaches to publicly recognize Jesus. Anna, too, has a deep spirituality cultivated through continual fasting and praying. In this brief encounter, we learn that in their long faithfulness, Simeon and Anna cultivated such a deep connection to the Spirit that they knew immediately when the Spirit stirred, even when it seemed irrational. Through decades of prayer, they had cultivated a wisdom that only elders could hold. As spiritual elders of the community, their role was to acknowledge Jesus's birth, prophesy over his life, serve as witnesses for the community, and prepare Mary's heart for her journey ahead as a mother.

The West tends to value the strength and energy of the young over the wisdom of elders. Many non-Western cultures, however, hold a communal posture centered around our community elders. Asian cultures observe ingrained, embodied practices for honoring elders, such as bowing, giving gifts, and offering the seat of honor at the table. A spirituality that holds the wisdom of our elders is a cyclical relationship of giving honor to our elders while also receiving their blessings.

Multigenerational Households

One of my earliest memories of Sunday school is singing "Jesus Loves Me" in Taiwanese. In the immigrant church, the purpose of Sunday school is to learn about Jesus and, at the same time, to learn about our culture. It wasn't until decades later that it suddenly occurred to me that the Taiwanese translation of "Jesus Loves Me" doesn't use the most common word for love, *ai*, 愛. Instead of using the word *ai*, the translators used a different term, *tia*, 疼. There is not an equivalent word for *tia* in English. *Tia* is specifically used to describe a parent's love for a child or to describe the care and attention from anyone older to someone younger, such as a grandparent's love or an older sibling's attentive care. The term connotes the actions and practices of caring for those you love, so it is usually mistranslated as "care" instead of "love." Oddly, the word *tia* can also mean "pain." One can discern whether you're referring to love or pain only from the context of the sentence. This double meaning seems to imply that this kind of love requires sacrifices and inherently comes with seasons of pain. Western culture taught me that love is expressed verbally by telling our loved ones "I love you." The Taiwanese express love through action and sacrifice. *Tia* brings me even deeper into the motherly and fatherly love of God. I wonder what else am I missing in my spirituality if I only use the English language to relate to God.

I grew up in a multigenerational household with my grandparents, and my many cousins, aunts, and uncles frequently came over. Sometimes a multigenerational home is a necessity for financial reasons, but many cultures value multigenerational homes, so they are a common non-Western practice. Children are expected to move out only when they marry and are ready to start their own families. Aging parents later move in with their adult children, who are honored to reciprocate an active love to their parents. As my grandparents took care of me, my parents took care of my grandparents. I also observed the many ways my grandparents were honored in the family.

As a high introvert, I know that communal living can be agitating, distracting, and draining. Multigenerational homes are full of activity from morning until evening. Navigating the kitchen is like a dance. Often, we are taught the spiritual life through practices of solitude and silence, but what if you live in a multigenerational home where privacy is not possible? In the West, we do not think of multigenerational households as a spiritual practice, but looking back, I realize that living in a lively home is actually a formative experience that has become an important part of my spiritual posture today. For me, living in a multigenerational home and taking care of my parents as they age is more important than having the privilege of independence or quiet. So I've come to see my daily interactions with my family as just as formative as solitude and silence.

Living in a full home brings about both an unforming and re-forming. The unforming work means practicing living with the particularities of others, confronting the unhealthiness in others and in myself. Unforming means doing the hard work of communicating, loving, and setting boundaries. And for those who have the privilege and option, unforming may be discerning when it is time to move out. Re-forming, on the other hand, includes learning to listen, honor, and celebrate together. Re-forming means being interruptible and allowing our plans to suddenly change to help someone else. Re-forming means learning to find our inner quiet and calm even if there's constant noise and the house is always a mess. Those who grow up in a culture of big families with many grandparents, aunts, uncles, and cousins are better able to understand that we are unavoidably connected by an interdependent web of relationships. Those relationships are part of our formation.

Also missing in Western spirituality is the spiritual posture of taking care of our parents as they age. Taking care of our parents may just be an obligation or expectation, but it becomes a spiritual posture when it begins with an intentional decision to love and honor our elders. Although many of us may go through this season, this practice is not often addressed in the Western church and especially not as a spiritual practice. As adults, many of us have to renavigate our changing relationships with our parents. In this posture, we intentionally accompany our parents, aunts, and uncles as they (and we) confront their aging and death. We learn to be present to our parents as their bodies fail them and their community dwindles. We are present as they encounter different kinds of loss and grief. This is not an easy practice. It can be very taxing on our physical bodies, minds, and souls. We are humbled as we help our parents with simple tasks that they can no longer do. In this practice, our souls become more attuned to our own mortality and fragile bodies. This spiritual season may last for an unexpected few weeks or for decades. Through it, we are formed in the cyclical life and what it means to age well when it is our turn.

Grieve Loudly, Grieve Together

We continue to honor our elders even when they die and become our ancestors. Many modern cultures are death avoidant. We created a funeral industry so we no longer have to prepare or interact with the lifeless body of the deceased. We avoid sitting and being with people who are facing death or with those who are grieving. Instead, we give them space and leave them alone. When we keep grief private, however, we are robbed of the healing power of grief.

The funeral practices in many non-Western cultures teach us grief is a communal experience. I have vivid memories of funeral processions in Taiwan, where grieving is public. When a beloved family member dies, the family sets up a street-side vigil for the deceased that can last for several days or even weeks. In this way, the vigil is shared with the whole neighborhood. I may pass by a bereaving family on the way to work or when picking up dinner. I cannot ignore the grief of my neighbors. Taiwanese funerals are also not quiet. The most vivid experience of grief takes place when the deceased body is ready to be cremated. The loud sounds of wailing and moaning fill the air as the family sends away their beloved family member to the fire. Sometimes professional wailers are hired to bring this last moment to a crescendo. The professional wailers communally express what the grieving family already feels so deeply inside. Their loud wailing frees the family and friends to wail as loudly as they need without being self-conscious. In these practices, the body expresses her grief loudly, and the community helps one another grieve.

Sometimes our hardest experiences of community are within our own families. We are so closely tied to our families that they can also be the ones who hurt us most. The people who know us most intimately are also those who know all our flaws and weaknesses. For those in collectivist cultures, familial ties and obligations include all our extended families too. As the church has developed in an individualist culture, we have neglected how much our families are part of our everyday formation. Thus, we need spiritual practices that help us engage the unforming and re-forming that we experience in our families.

For Reflection and Discussion

1. In what ways are elders honored in your culture?
2. What are your own formative experiences in multigenerational households or caring for your aging parents?
3. What family stories or wisdoms did your grandparents, parents, or elders share with you?
4. How does your culture grieve?

9

HARMONY

I believe that our collective soul is struggling ultimately because we have become numb to our collective sufferings. Only with an individualistic faith can we disconnect someone else's suffering from our own. When we disassociate from the injustices and disparities of our times, our souls begin to erode. When we prioritize individual freedom over the life and well-being of others, we lose, little by little, our own humanity. Each individual decision we make to ignore and turn away is a decision that harms the whole. Indifference to the suffering of others is a decision to not see the sacred in another human being.

Our suffering is and has always been collective, but we lose this truth in the church when we disconnect our faith from our responsibility to take care of the suffering and oppressed. Gustavo Gutiérrez wrote, "For each of us our sorrows are deeply personal. For all of us our sorrows, too, are universal."[1] Just as Jesus held the sufferings of the world in his body on the cross, we also need to learn to hold our collective suffering as our own.

Suffering is such a deeply embodied and communal experience, and I am discovering different cultures use different idioms, expressions, or metaphors to try to capture

the depth of our suffering. In Chinese, the term for suffering is *chi ku*, 吃苦, which literally means "eating bit-
terness," implying that suffering has a taste and is ingested
into our bodies. In Korean, suffering is expressed with the
word *han*. Theologian Grace Ji-Sun Kim explains that *han*
refers specifically to unresolved "unjust suffering."[2] She
writes, "Han is the suffering when the social, political, and
religious system is set up to oppress, dominate, and subju-
gate another or groups of people." *Han* is then a suffering
that is shared and experienced by a community of people.
Han is also a suffering perpetuated collectively through systems. To address *han*, we have to collectively address the
injustices of history.

Ada María Isasi-Díaz writes that for Latin American
women, the more fitting term in Spanish is not one we
translate as "suffering" but a word typically translated as
"the struggle," *la lucha*. She writes, "Even in the moments of
greatest suffering in our lives, if looked at from below and
from within, the suffering is not what is most influential
in determining how we act, talk, make decisions. Though
Hispanic women suffer racial/ethnic and sexist oppression
and most of us also suffer poverty, we do not go about our
vida cotidiana—our everyday life—thinking that we suffer but rather thinking how to struggle to survive, to live
fully."[3] The everyday struggle of Latin American women
demonstrates for us a posture of staying and surviving with
the community in the midst of suffering. These and other
words for "suffering" create a more complex understanding
of our communal suffering and the different ways we can
carry our sufferings together.

In an individualist society, we are not taught a posture of how to carry our collective suffering. Theologian
Dorothee Soelle writes of our modern culture, "Whoever

deals with his suffering only in the way our society has taught him—through illusion, minimization, suppression, apathy—will deal with societal suffering in the same way."[4] We need a spiritual posture that helps us stay present to the sufferings of others even in our discomfort and resist our urges to ignore or separate ourselves from the community.

In the Gospels, the women at the cross teach us this important spiritual posture of witnessing and staying with the suffering community. When the Romans take Jesus in for interrogation and then publicly sentence him to death by crucifixion, most of his disciples desert him. They are afraid. Their minds begin to spin with questions. What happens to Jesus's vision and role as a leader in the movement? How can he possibly save us now? Why did we waste all these years following him? They scatter out of fear and disillusionment because they cannot reconcile their theological understanding of Jesus with this unexpected turn of events. The religious movement they are trying to build collapses. But the Gospels tell us that a group of women stay with Jesus. Women with no voice and no power choose to do what others don't: they accompany Jesus to the cross. They are present as he dies; they are still there when he is buried. Perhaps these women also feel the same disappointment and doubt and ask the same questions as the other disciples, but more important than their mental questioning is their love for a friend. In their fears, they witness Jesus's desperate cry on the cross and hear his last breath because they love him. In their grief, they prepare the spices and fragrances to tend to his dead body because they love him. Jesus can no longer do anything for them, but that doesn't matter. They want to do something for Jesus. In a time of fear, pain, and grief, they stay anyway to be present to Jesus and to one another.

Every year during holy week, I copy the short verses in the Gospels that refer to the women at the cross, and I paste together their story. I center the story of the women because they were the only ones who actually witnessed the whole thing. By staying, they demonstrate the power of witness. Because they stay, the women of the cross also become the first witnesses to a new kind of life, resurrection.

I need to be formed by the collective spirituality of the women at the cross so that I don't run away from the sufferings in my community. As we experience natural disasters, pandemics, violence, and mass killings as a community, we need a posture of staying together. We need to learn to grieve and gather for vigils together, to watch over and take care of one another, to speak up as witnesses of injustices, and to march and protest together. To stay with those who are suffering is a spiritual practice of solidarity.

The Sin of Disharmony

In individualistic cultures, we tend to view sin as a list of personal bad behaviors, choices, and morals. Whether we define sin as missing the mark, the original sin of Adam, or comparing ourselves to the holiness of God, we tend to view these definitions through the lens of self rather than the collective. Sins are my own decision, and therefore, the consequences are my own to bear. This individualistic view of sin makes it easy for us to excuse ourselves from the sufferings of others. Under this understanding of sin, I am responsible only for myself, a view that then contributes to our collective apathy and indifference toward the suffering in our communities. So even though the church, particularly the evangelical church, can become obsessed with individual sins, we are blind to our collective and societal, even global, sins.

Social anthropologist Melba Padilla Maggay teaches us a non-Western definition of sin as "social disharmony."[5] Rather than viewing sin as individual choices that only affect ourselves, she argues that sin involves our relationships to the community. Sin is breaking our trust and responsibilities to our immediate community as well as the community of all creation. An understanding of sin as social disharmony is much more in line with the Old Testament focus on the breaking of relationship and covenant. God's anger is directed at those who have oppressed the foreigner, fatherless, and widow (Ezek 22). The neglect of the Sabbath is a sin because it perpetuates an economic system that harms the whole. Padilla Maggay writes that this collective view of sin conveys "the sense that a whole community is responsible for the breakdown of life systems."[6] Sin is collective because our individual actions always affect the greater whole. The community must bear the consequences of individual and collective decisions. When we as individuals, as a church, or as a nation make a harmful decision, we are breaking our interconnectedness. Therefore, the consequence of our collective sin is our collective responsibility to repair and restore. Even if my individual behavior may not directly lead to our broken systems, I am still responsible for responding to the suffering, racism, inequality, and oppression that our collective sins, our systems, have created.

A collective definition of sin creates a collective understanding of justice. The West understands justice through a law-based system in which justice is served when one individual is punished for wrongdoing. This way of justice, however, disregards those who were harmed, who continue to carry the pain and consequences of injustice for the rest of their lives. Sometimes the consequences of injustices are carried for generations. An individualistic understanding of justice will never motivate us to repair the harm done to our Black and Indigenous communities. A relational understanding of justice means we all carry the responsibility for making things right.

To address our collective sins, we need the spiritual posture of harmony—the practice of restoring right relationships. Desmond Tutu writes, "Social harmony is for us the *summum bonum*—the greatest good."[7] The notion of harmony as the ultimate good is also found in both Asian philosophies and Indigenous traditions. Randy Woodley proposes that the way of harmony found in Indigenous cultures is the same as the biblical concept of shalom.[8] Harmony or shalom is the process of restoration; it is our collective and ongoing work with God. Harmony is the spiritual posture that will heal our collective soul.

Our initial understanding of harmony may be to compromise or avoid conflict, but this is a distorted understanding of harmony. In patriarchal cultures, harmony can be misused to cover up the wrongdoings of those in power by forcing those who are abused to ignore the harm done to them for the sake of the community. Especially in shame-based cultures, harmony can be misused to silence people. Harmony, however, does not mean being agreeable. In fact, harmony may sometimes mean being angry when relationships are abused.

Anger

To repair and restore our social disharmony, we need the spiritual practice of anger. Desert Father Isaiah the Solitary believed that we need anger in our prayers. He writes, "Without anger a man cannot attain purity; he has to feel angry with all that is sown in him by the enemy."[9] BIPOC communities need to be angry with all that has been stolen from us. That anger is part of the holy and sacred work of unforming. Creator of Black liturgies Cole Arthur Riley writes, "Holy anger is that which liberates. It marches, chants, and flips tables, demanding wrong be called by its rightful name. It is both passion and calculation, longing for more but for the sake of justice and dignity."[10] Anger is the only spiritual practice powerful enough to disarm our collective and systemic sins, because we need to hate these sins in order to undo the social disharmony they cause. For the oppressed, God's anger in the Scriptures is comforting. God's anger demonstrates that God is not indifferent to our sufferings.

Adopting a posture of anger means acknowledging I, too, am responsible for our racist and oppressive social systems even if I may be a victim of such systems. I must grapple with systems that destroy Black and Indigenous communities. To engage with my soul work, I must be angry when a Black life is unjustly taken, when Indigenous lands continue to be stolen, and when those looking for safety at the border are turned away, just as I am angry when an Asian body is assaulted for being foreign. For BIPOC communities, especially, healing begins with being angry at the lies that dehumanize us and the dignity that has been taken from us.

Throughout my life, I have worked in several white organizations. When I sit in endless conversations about diversifying an organization with predominately white leaders, I am often most bothered by the lack of anger in our discussions. Although white Christian leaders may be educating themselves about race and have good intentions for our meetings, their lack of anger demonstrates to me that they still do not see racism as *our* problem. They approach injustices with the intention to fix the problem without truly acknowledging and lamenting the harm done.

After the back-to-back killings of Ahmaud Arbery, Breonna Taylor, and George Floyd in 2020 and the countless Black lives before and after, a good friend of mine, Pastor Hannah, led our community in an embodied, communal, and public reading of the book of Lamentations. We were asked to take a long walk in the city as we listened together on our phones to a full reading of Lamentations. Hearing the ancient words of anger and blame at God in the context of current events seemed to speak prophetically to our time. As I listened to the words, I was reminded that the practice of lament includes rage as much as grief. As I walked, I could feel my body swell with our collective disillusionment and hopelessness. Walking through my own neighborhood with the angry prayers ringing in my ears helped me notice the suffering and injustices in my own community. This communal spiritual practice of reading Lamentations was one of the most memorable spiritual practices I have ever experienced. It allowed me to wrestle with our collective injustices. It allowed our community to stay together in our disillusionment, even as we offered no words of comfort or false theologies of hope. In those times, when we are so upset that we cannot pray, we allow our emotions to be our prayers. We pray through grief and anger, and that is enough.

To embrace harmony means to acknowledge, carry together, and bear witness to the sufferings of others. When those bearing the weight of injustice have no more energy to be angry and no more tears to mourn, the community continues to grieve and rage for and with them. When we march on the streets, we share our collective anger. When we gather for vigils on the sidewalk, we experience our collective grief. When we weep privately in our own homes for people we may have never met, we express our collective lament. Harmony is our collective effort to make right our broken, distorted, unjust, and abusive relationships. Harmony also means holding our leaders accountable to use their power to repair social harm and restore harmony. Harmony also involves living in right relationship with the earth and creation, as creation too is our community. Harmony can never be maintained alone; it must be a communal posture. We need to take care of and take responsibility for one another, for our communities, for our systems, and for the earth.

For Reflection and Discussion

1. What collective sufferings do you hold for the world at this time?
2. Defining sin as social disharmony rather than bad behavior, how do you think you have contributed to the collective sins of our communities?
3. How have you been affected by our collective sins?
4. Have you engaged with the spiritual practice of anger? How did you do that?

CONCLUSION

As I wrote this book, I asked myself this primary question in each chapter: How do we as people of color take care of our souls? BIPOC communities are weary from constantly trying to contort ourselves into a Western way of being not created for us. We get worn down by everyday realities as we navigate through white-dominated systems. We experience this weariness in the church just as much as anywhere else. The spiritual life is cultivating the inner sustainability we need to navigate our world, and BIPOC people often find this world denies our humanity and belonging. When I think about why spirituality is so important, I often recall Barbara Holmes's words on the spirituality of those who participated in the civil rights movement. She writes, "You cannot face German shepherds and fire hoses without your own resources, there must be God and stillness at the very center of your being."[1] We need a deeply rooted spirituality in order to sustain our souls and our bodies for all the work required to take care of our collective well-being.

Sustaining resilience, resistance, and survival skills, however, are exhausting practices. We also need a spiritual life that moves us beyond the practices of surviving, resilience, and resistance to one of rest and creativity. I am not asking us, however, to retreat or get away from our lives in order to find rest. Not all in our communities have the

privilege of doing that. We cannot run away from our collective suffering and injustices. So I am asking us to stay. I
invite us to live deeper into the messiness of life and community in order to find our rest and creativity within it. A
rhythm of finding temporary respite or soothing our overworked bodies, only to go back after a break into the same
oppressive and depleted conditions, is not spiritual formation. We must be transformed in our evolving spirituality
to discover a new way of being in this world, a sustained
rest, and a different way of community. We need a communal imagination to create our ways of rest right here in our
communities and our everyday lives.

Although I have studied Christian spirituality for a
long time, I realize that I can never become an expert on
spirituality, because spirituality happens in our daily experiences with God, not through study or self-discipline. In
the end, the spiritual life is not just formed in the crisis
moments when we may need God most. Instead, our spirituality is also experienced through the mundane, ordinary
days. Our most routine, uneventful days are when our
spirituality, our divine-human interaction, is happening,
although we are often unaware. Spirituality is the way we
connect our everyday lives to the divine. It is that deep
longing to experience the sacredness of life, self, God, community, and the earth. Spirituality facilitates a deep seeing
and knowing, so we might see ourselves, God, and others as God sees. We then carry this sacred seeing into our
day-to-day lives in order to see and experience sacredness
everywhere.

What hinders spirituality most is rarely bad habits but
indifference. We may find it easier to be numb to this life
and to this world. To attend to our souls, we need to exam-
ine our whole selves to find where our hearts have grown

calloused. To cultivate our spirituality is to come alive again. Thus, we need to adopt intentional spiritual postures that help us enter into our everyday formation with intention and awareness of the movements of the sacred all around. It is our spirituality in the ordinary days that determines how we respond when the unexpected happens. And in those times when unexpected events require action, courage, and strength, the sacred moments formed and layered in the ordinary days sustain us through seasons of greater uncertainty.

Our daily encounters with God are not always easy. We are brought into just as many seasons of unforming as re-forming. Our unforming is an unraveling of all the ways our perceptions of self, God, and one another have become distorted. This unforming includes how the Western church has forced us to conform to white Western values, ideologies, and systems. We unform layers of injustices and oppression built up throughout our history. We unform not just for ourselves but for our elders and generations past. In Mirabai Starr's translation of *Dark Night of the Soul*, she suggests that we may enter seasons of spiritual disillusionment and emptiness because our old constructions of God need to be stripped away in order for us to experience God anew.[2] I believe that we are collectively moving into such a season as we become more and more disillusioned by our traditional patriarchal institutions of church. There is so much more of God that we don't know yet and haven't experienced, but we're afraid of letting go of the God who was handed to us. So our unforming continues as we take a risk and let go in order to give God space to reveal to us the God we may not know.

Even as our unforming continues, we also prepare for our communal re-forming. I believe that the work of re-forming is communal, not individual. I also believe re-forming is the mighty work of the Spirit if we allow her the freedom to move. So I conclude here with three spiritual movements that prepare us for this sacred re-forming.

Cultivating Spaciousness

In order for the creative and divine Spirit to do her work, we need to have spaciousness within ourselves and in our communities. Our ongoing spiritual practices and postures of rest, stillness, and listening nurture this spaciousness. Spaciousness helps us enter into life with an open posture. Through cultivating spaciousness, we make more room for ourselves even as the world may try to suppress our sacred selves. And when we experience spaciousness within our own lives, we also create spaciousness for others. In return, a healthy community also nurtures my inner spaciousness. When my community reflects to me my sacredness, they unclutter the other voices that may deny my sacredness.

Trusting Our Intuitions

This spaciousness is not empty or nothing. It is a space carefully cultivated for us by our ancestors through their embodied, often subversive spiritualities. The Western church taught us that "tradition" refers to the authority of white male theologians and their interpretations of Scripture. For non-Western communities, however, tradition refers to the wisdoms of our generations past. Our ancestors taught us a way of being counter to the Western colonial way of being. We can trust our communal wisdoms as we carry that tradition in our own bodies. As we remove each layer in the unforming work, we begin to access our most honest and raw selves to experience God most directly. Our spirituality comes out of this sacred space where we meet with God. This direct experience is not filtered through a white lens and not regulated by those in power. In that space, we can trust our intuitions and how the Spirit moves and speaks within us. We come to know God not from books or authorities but through encounter. In our re-forming, we trust our knowings of God as well as our ancestral ways of knowing.

Embracing Our Collective Spirituality

A private, individualized spirituality is not sufficient. If we care about only our own rest and self-care, then the transforming power of spirituality is limited to only ourselves. I believe the spirituality we need in our times is one that embraces our shared bodies and collective spirit to acknowledge that we're inextricably tied to one another. We can embrace the reality that in our collective soul, we can feel one another's pain. In a collective spirituality, we are formed to carry our burdens together. When tragedy comes, we all carry the heaviness of grief. When someone in our community is murdered, we all feel that pain in our own bodies. Thus we can mourn deeply for the loss of those we may never have met. Some of us are more aware of our interconnectedness than others. Some of us are completely oblivious. In our re-forming, we attend to our deeply wounded and debilitated communities in order to heal our collective soul.

I truly believe that if women, if people of color, if queer
theologians had led the way in our spirituality, how we
experience, practice, and engage with the sacred would
look radically different. How we gather in community
would look different. How we interpret and interact with
the Scriptures would be different. Our practices and rituals would feel different. So let's find out together what a
non-Western, nonpatriarchal spirituality looks like. What
does it smell, taste, sound, and feel like in our bodies? I
hope these initial nine spiritual postures feel more natural
for BIPOC communities as we embrace the ways that our
families and communities taught us. Western spirituality
emphasizes spiritual formation as a set of practices and
actions rather than our ways of being in the world. But
spirituality is not something we put into our schedules or
understand with our minds. We embody it with our being.
Thus, the wisdoms of our cultures matter in how we interact with God. Our cultural ways of moving and feeling our
bodies, our cultural ways of perceiving life and what we
value all matter in how we connect with God. Our conversations are just starting. I look forward to hearing from you,
about your spiritual postures, and about the God you know.

Notes

Introduction

1. Howard Thurman, *The Creative Encounter* (Richmond, IN: Friends United, 1972), 39.
2. Karen Baker-Fletcher, *Dancing with God: The Trinity from a Womanist Perspective* (Nashville: Chalice, 2006), 55.
3. Desmond Tutu, *God Has a Dream: A Vision of Hope for Our Time* (New York: Image Books, 2004), 50.

Part 1: Orientation → Cyclical

1. Kaiping Peng, Julie Spencer-Rodgers, and Zhong Nian, "Naïve Dialecticism and the Tao of Chinese Thought," in *Indigenous and Cultural Psychology*, ed. Uichol Kim, Kuo-Shu Yang, and Kwang-Kuo Hwang (New York: Springer, 2006), 247–62.
2. Li-Jin Ji, Richard E. Nisbett, and Yanjie Su, "Culture, Change, and Prediction," *Psychological Science* 12, no. 6 (November 2001): 450–56.
3. Derek Lew, trans., *Tao Te Ching: Annotated and Explained* (Woodstock, VT: Skylight Paths, 2006), 30.
4. Randy Woodley, *Shalom and the Community of Creation: An Indigenous Vision* (Grand Rapids, MI: Eerdmans, 2012), 88.

5. Steven Charleston, *Ladder to the Light: An Indigenous Elder's Meditations on Hope and Courage* (Minneapolis: Broadleaf, 2021), 67.

6. Chung Hyun Kyung, *Struggle to Be the Sun Again: Introducing Asian Women's Theology* (Maryknoll, NY: Orbis, 1994), 86.

7. Howard Thurman, *Deep River and the Negro Spiritual Speaks of Life and Death* (Richmond, IN: Friends United, 1975), 77.

8. Malcolm Muggeridge and Missionaries of Charity, *Something Beautiful for God: Mother Teresa of Calcutta* (London: Collins-Fount, 1977).

9. Barbara A. Holmes, *Joy Unspeakable: Contemplative Practices of the Black Church* (Minneapolis: Fortress, 2017), 2.

Chapter 1: Time

1. Donald P. McNeill et al., *Compassion: A Reflection on the Christian Life* (Garden City, NY: Doubleday, 1982), 97.

2. Yi Fu Tuan, *Romantic Geography: In Search of the Sublime Landscape* (Madison: University of Wisconsin Press, 2013), 113.

3. Melba Padilla Maggay, "A Religion of Guilt Encounters a Religion of Power," in *The Gospel in Culture: Contextualization Issues through Asian Eyes*, ed. Melba Padilla Maggay (Manila: OMF Literature, 2013), 54.

4. Maggay, 52.

Chapter 2: Remembering

1. Howard Thurman, *Jesus and the Disinherited* (Boston: Beacon, 1996).

2. Masako Ema Watanabe, "Styles of Explanation and Evaluation in History Education," *Journal of Educational Sociology* 73 (2003): 43–63.

3. Minkyung Koo, Jong An Choi, and Incheol Choi, "Analytic versus Holistic Cognition," in *The Psychological and Cultural Foundations of East Asian Cognition*, ed. Julie Spencer-Rodgers and Kaiping Peng (New York: Oxford University Press, 2018), 105–34.

4. Maurice J. Nutt, "A Sankofa Moment: Exploring a Genealogy of Justice," in *Ain't Gonna Let Nobody Turn Me Around*, ed. Therese Taylor-Stinson (New York: Church Publishing, 2017), loc. 2046 of 2331, Kindle.

5. Charleston, *Ladder to the Light*, 90.

Chapter 3: Uncertainty

1. Richard E. Nisbett, *The Geography of Thought: How Asians and Westerners Think Differently . . . and Why* (New York: Free Press, 2003), 25.

2. Gustavo Gutiérrez, *On Job: God Talk and the Suffering of the Innocent* (Maryknoll, NY: Orbis, 1987), xv.

3. James Cone, *The Spirituals and the Blues* (Maryknoll, NY: Orbis, 1991), 54.

4. Cone, 66.

5. Holmes, *Joy Unspeakable*, 50.

6. Peng, Spencer-Rodgers, and Nian, "Naïve Dialecticism."

7. Peng, Spencer-Rodgers, and Nian, 251.

8. Miguel De La Torre, *Embracing Hopelessness* (Minneapolis: Fortress, 2017), 95.

9. Anna More, ed., *Sor Juana Inés de la Cruz: Selected Works*, trans. Edith Grossman (New York: W. W. Norton, 2016), ballad 2.

10. Yi Fu Tuan, "Sense of Place," *American Journal of Theology and Philosophy* 18, no. 1 (1997): 52.

Part 2: Orientation ∴ Experience

1. Cláudio Carvalhaes, ed., *Liturgy in Postcolonial Perspectives: Only One Is Holy* (New York: Palgrave Macmillan, 2015), 4.
2. Giuseppe Giordan, "The Body between Religion and Spirituality," *Social Compass* 56, no. 2 (2009): 228.
3. Woodley, *Shalom and the Community*, 96.
4. Howard Thurman, *Howard Thurman: Essential Writings*, ed. Luther E. Smith Jr. (Maryknoll, NY: Orbis, 2006), 46.
5. Simon Chan, "Asian Christian Spirituality in Primal Religious Contexts," in Maggay, *Gospel in Culture*, 47.
6. Ada María Isasi-Díaz, *Mujerista Theology: A Theology for the Twenty-First Century* (Maryknoll, NY: Orbis, 1996), 86.
7. Carvalhaes, *Liturgy in Postcolonial Perspectives*, 6.
8. Constance Classen, *The Deepest Sense: A Cultural History of Touch* (Urbana: University of Illinois Press, 2012), 183.
9. Classen.
10. Isabel Wilkerson, *Caste: The Origins of Our Discontents* (New York: Random House, 2020).
11. Carvalhaes, *Liturgy in Postcolonial Perspectives*, 9.

Chapter 4: Imagination

1. Willie James Jennings, *The Christian Imagination: Theology and the Origins of Race* (New Haven, CT: Yale University Press, 2010), 6.
2. Christena Cleveland, *God Is a Black Woman* (New York: HarperOne, 2022), 16.
3. De La Torre, *Embracing Hopelessness*, 5.
4. De La Torre, 6.
5. Walter Brueggemann, *The Prophetic Imagination* (Minneapolis: Fortress, 1978), 40.
6. De La Torre, *Embracing Hopelessness*, 34.

Chapter 5: Language

1. Nisbett, *Geography of Thought*, 60.
2. Herbert Moyo, "Liturgy and Justice in Postcolonial Zimbabwe: Holy People, Holy Places, Holy Things in the Evangelical Lutheran Church in Zimbabwe," in Carvalhaes, *Liturgy in Postcolonial Perspectives*, 97.
3. Nell Irvin Painter, *Sojourner Truth: A Life, a Symbol* (New York: W. W. Norton, 1996), 86.
4. Painter, 225.
5. Gutiérrez, *On Job*, xiv.
6. Thomas Merton, *The Wisdom of the Desert: Sayings from the Desert Fathers of the Fourth Century* (New York: New Directions, 1961), 20.

Chapter 6: Work/Rest

1. Gustavo Gutiérrez, *We Drink from Our Own Wells: The Spiritual Journey of a People* (Maryknoll, NY: Orbis, 2003), 14.
2. Brueggemann, *Prophetic Imagination*, 6.
3. Brueggemann, 27.
4. Brueggemann, 17.
5. Brueggemann, 30.
6. Woodley, *Shalom and the Community*, 30.
7. Walter Brueggemann, *Sabbath as Resistance: Saying No to the Culture of Now* (Louisville, KY: Westminster John Knox, 2014), 15.
8. Abraham Heschel, *Sabbath: Its Meaning for Modern Man* (New York: Farrar, Straus & Giroux, 2005), 32.
9. Thurman, *Howard Thurman*, 60.

Part 3: Orientation ⊒ Collective

1. Woodley, *Shalom and the Community*, chap. 7.

2. Jeanne Halgren Kilde, *When Church Became Theatre: The Transformation of Evangelical Architecture and Worship in Nineteenth-Century America* (New York: Oxford University Press, 2002), 17.
3. Jennings, *Christian Imagination*, 8.

Chapter 7: Dependence

1. Nisbett, *Geography of Thought*, 50.
2. William S. Gray, *Fun with Dick and Jane* (Chicago: Scott, Foresman, 1930).
3. Nisbett, *Geography of Thought*, 50.
4. Gutiérrez, *We Drink*, 15.
5. Michael Battle, "Ubuntu: Learning from the African Worldview," *Sewanee Theological Review* 53, no. 4 (2010): 404.
6. Gutiérrez, *We Drink*, 110.
7. Gustavo Gutiérrez, *Spiritual Writings*, ed. Daniel G. Groody (Maryknoll, NY: Orbis, 2011), 68.
8. Tutu, *God Has a Dream*, 25.
9. Chuang Tzu, *Chuang Tzu: Selections Annotated and Explained*, trans. Livia Kohn (Woodstock, VT: Skylight Paths, 2011), chap. 2.

Chapter 8: Elders

1. Kat Armas, *Abuelita Faith: What Women on the Margins Teach Us about Wisdom, Persistence, and Strength* (Grand Rapids, MI: Brazos, 2021), 33.
2. Carolina Hinojosa-Cisneros, "We Survive by Telling Stories," *On Being* (blog), May 14, 2018, https://onbeing.org/blog/carolina-hinojosa-cisneros-we-survive-by-telling-stories/.
3. Isasi-Díaz, *Mujerista Theology*, 70.

Chapter 9: Harmony

1. Gutiérrez, *On Job*, 34.
2. Grace Ji-Sun Kim, *Embracing the Other* (Grand Rapids, MI: Eerdmans, 2015), chap. 2.
3. Isasi-Díaz, *Mujerista Theology*, 66.
4. Dorothee Soelle, *Suffering* (Minneapolis: Fortress, 1984), 4.
5. Maggay, *Gospel in Culture*, 38.
6. Maggay, 39.
7. Tutu, *God Has a Dream*, 27.
8. Tutu, xv.
9. Makarios Nicodemus, G. E. H. Sherrard Palmer, and Philip Kallistos, eds., *The Philokalia: The Complete Text*, vol. 1 (Boston: Faber & Faber, 1979), 22.
10. Cole Arthur Riley, *This Here Flesh: Spirituality, Liberation, and the Stories That Make Us* (New York: Convergent, 2022), 118.

Conclusion

1. Holmes, *Joy Unspeakable*, 116.
2. John of the Cross, *Dark Night of the Soul*, trans. Mirabai Starr (New York: Riverhead, 2002).

Recommended Resources

There are so many BIPOC theologians doing good work that I wish I could list them all. I continue my effort of trying to read them all. I offer here a short list of authors who stirred creativity in me as I was researching and writing this book. Each of these authors expresses a deep personal spirituality that comes from within their embodied experiences of God and is not restricted by Western parameters. They each pushed me in different ways to look deeper into my own spirituality and to break free from the boundaries of how we traditionally define and experience spirituality.

Armas, Kat. *Abuelita Faith: What Women on the Margins Teach Us about Wisdom, Persistence, and Strength* (Brazos, 2021)

> I deeply miss my grandma while reading this book. Through this book, Armas brings us into her *abuelita*'s kitchen and reveals to us the deep theology we can learn from our grandmothers. As she looks at Scripture through the lens of her lived experience, Armas beautifully expresses her Latina spirituality.

Charleston, Steven. *Ladder to the Light: An Indigenous Elder's Meditations on Hope and Courage* (Broadleaf, 2021)

> I can't tell if this book is one of poetry, prayer, or wisdom. It feels like all three. Through his slow, thoughtful

reflections, Charleston expresses the deep wisdom of his Indigenous spirituality. As I read each meditation, I feel like I am standing right beside Charleston as he stands outside to greet the earth and receive these prayers each morning.

Chung Hyun Kyung. *Struggle to Be the Sun Again: Introducing Asian Women's Theology* (Orbis, 1994)

Chung Hyun Kyung's writing gives me the courage to not be afraid. She makes me feel powerful. In this book, she draws together the voices and experiences of Asian women and presents our beautiful, unique spirituality to the world. She reminds us that women carry a cosmic religion in our own bodies that our male-dominated religions do not recognize.

Cleveland, Christena. *God Is a Black Woman* (HarperOne, 2022)

In this book, Cleveland takes us with her on a spiritual pilgrimage to visit the Black Madonna in her many forms. This is one of the most life-transforming books I have ever read. Cleveland changed the way I see and imagine. She brought me closer to God by sharing her own personal experience with God as a Black woman. I think all of us need to read this book to transform our collective imagination.

Curtice, Kaitlin B. *Native: Identity, Belonging, and Rediscovering God* (Brazos, 2020)

In this book, Curtice tells the difficult story of Indigenous peoples in the United States through her own personal story. These are stories we all need to listen to. Curtice beautifully integrates Indigenous storytelling, spirituality, culture, and history.

De La Torre, Miguel A. *Embracing Hopelessness* (Fortress, 2017)
   This book stirred up a holy anger in me. De La Torre
   powerfully weaves our global history of oppression
   with our false, empty theologies of hope. He recognized
   the part in me, in us, that feels hopeless and shows a
   more powerful way through a spirituality of hopelessness. I don't know how to adequately summarize this
   book. Just read it.

Gutiérrez, Gustavo. *We Drink from Our Own Wells: The Spiritual Journey of a People* (Orbis, 2003)
   I am always amazed that the man known as the
   father of liberation theology had such a deep contemplative spirituality. But perhaps it shouldn't surprise
   me that a theology of liberation for the poor, particularly those in Latin America, must have a deep contemplative experience at the very center of that liberation.

Holmes, Barbara A. *Joy Unspeakable: Contemplative Practices
   of the Black Church* (Fortress, 2017)
   I read this book three times and will continue to
   return to this work again and again. Holmes was the
   first to show me that there could be a spirituality completely outside the confines of a Western spirituality. She
   writes particularly of the Black experience of God and
   the deep spirituality reflected in rituals and activism.

Jennings, Willie James. *The Christian Imagination: Theology
   and the Origins of Race* (Yale University Press, 2010).
   For those looking for a theological discourse on
   decolonizing our Christian faith, this book is the place
   to start. Jennings uses a historical lens to pinpoint
   and analyze the ways that Western Christianity distorted our social imaginations. This book provides a

helpful foundation and framework for the theology that informs a non-Western spirituality.

Riley, Cole Arthur. *This Here Flesh: Spirituality, Liberation, and the Stories That Make Us* (Convergent, 2022)

Cole Arthur Riley is the voice we need for our times. And indeed, her voice came to our awareness during the pandemic as she led us to breathe and pray. In her own contemplative way, she shows us a way of spirituality, leadership, and writing that centers the Black experience.

Thurman, Howard. *The Creative Encounter* (Friends United, 1972)

If I could, I would list here all of Thurman's books. As a fellow mystic and academic, I find in Thurman a kindred spirit and wise elder. I highlight this particular book because in it, Thurman addresses our direct experiences of God and how our inner experiences might lead to an embodied, loving presence in the world.

Woodley, Randy. *Shalom and the Community of Creation: An Indigenous Vision* (Eerdmans, 2012)

As I read Woodley's Indigenous, earth-rooted spirituality, I too felt a connection to the earth and a longing for a different kind of spirituality. Interestingly, I discovered through this book that there are many similarities between Indigenous ways of being and Daoist ways of being. I suppose Indigenous wisdom and spirituality from long ago is also a universal wisdom, since it comes from our relationships to the earth.